WADE COOK'S POWER QUOTES

Volume One

WADE COOK'S
POWER QUOTES

Volume One

Wade B. Cook

Lighthouse Publishing Group, Inc.
Seattle, Washington

LIGHTHOUSE PUBLISHING GROUP, INC.
PORTIONS COPYRIGHT © 1998 WADE B. COOK

Library of Congress Cataloging-in-Publication Data
Cook, Wade B.
Wade Cook's Power Quotes
Volume One
p. cm.
ISBN: 0-910019-90-8 (alk. paper)
I. Quotations, English.   I. Title.
PN6081.C588   1998
082--dc21   98-28818   CIP

Lighthouse Publishing Group, Inc. would like to thank the following people for their invaluable help, without which Wade Cook's Power Quotes would not be possible:

Executive Director: Cheryle Hamilton
Production Directors: Brent Magarrell, Alison Curtis
Promotion Director: Jerry Miller
Book Design: Judy Burkhalter
Dust Jacket Design: Cynthia Fliege
Editing and Proofing: Bethany McVannel, K. Noel Thomas, Kathryn Drinkard,
        Diana Imhoff, Carolyn Norris

Published by:
Lighthouse Publishing Group, Inc.
14675 Interurban Avenue South
Seattle, Washington 98168-4664
1-800-706-8657   206-901-3100 (fax)
www.lighthousebooks.com
Source code: WCCQ98

Printed in the United States of America
10 9 8 7 6 5 4 3 2 1

To Brenda, Cody, and Ashley Laura,
my oldest daughter and her family.

To Carrie, Donnie, and Braydon,
my second daughter and her family.

To Leslie, Rachel, and Ben,
the three we still have at home.

And to Laura,
my wonderful wife and mother of these children.
She loves them more than life itself and shares
the abundant lessons of life with them unselfishly.

I love you all, and pray always that
God may attend you in all you do.

OTHER BOOKS BY
LIGHTHOUSE PUBLISHING GROUP, INC.

Wealth 101, Wade Cook

Brilliant Deductions, Wade Cook

The Secret Millionaire Guide to Nevada Corporations
John Childers, Jr.

Millions Heirs, John Childers, Jr.

Bear Market Baloney, Wade Cook

Blueprints for Success, Volume I, Various Authors

Rolling Stocks, Gregory Witt

Sleeping Like A Baby, John Hudelson

Stock Market Miracles, Wade Cook

Wall Street Money Machine, Wade Cook

101 Ways To Buy Real Estate Without Cash, Wade Cook

Cook's Book On Creative Real Estate, Wade Cook

How To Pick Up Foreclosures, Wade Cook

Owner Financing, Wade Cook

Real Estate Money Machine, Wade Cook

Real Estate For Real People, Wade Cook

A+, Wade Cook

Business Buy The Bible, Wade Cook

Don't Set Goals, Wade Cook

Living In Color, Renae Knapp

CONTENTS

If you'll do for a few years what most people won't do, you'll be able to do for the rest of your life what most people can't do.

Wade B. Cook

PREFACE

About the age of 14, I became acutely aware of powerful sayings by people all over the world. Most of the authors had passed on long before, yet I couldn't quit reading their sayings.

When I was a junior in high school, my teacher put a saying up every few days in the corner of the chalkboard. I really liked them and started my own collection. I'll give you an idea of how they have changed my life. I have been successful beyond my wildest dreams. Many people ask who, or what, drives me, or what influences I've had? There are many turning points in all of our lives—almost demarcation lines, points of change that make us substantially different.

One such time for me was when I was 14, almost 15. There was a convergence in my life of two great parents, wonderful church leaders, a schoolteacher, my thoughtful brothers and sisters, and my own determination to not be poor. I attended Lincoln High School in Tacoma, Washington. All class pictures from the early 1900's were displayed all the way down the main hall. I think each had their class slogan in the bottom of the pictures. One slogan, I think it was 1917, said "If there's a way, take it; if not, make it." This statement had a big impact on me. Since then it has permeated so much of what I have done. It still means a lot to me.

Back then books by Napoleon Hill (Think & Grow Rich), Dale Carnegie (How to Win Friends and Influence People), and James Allen (As a Man Thinketh) were popular. These books and sayings meant the world to me.

Oh, don't get me wrong, my parents raised me with the Bible as a main stay in our home, and they made sure I was at Sunday School every Sunday. I had memorized dozens, if not hundreds of scriptures. Funny how these scriptures can be read and memorized in one's head, but how hard it is to live them and have them permeate your life. That requires buying into them in your heart, not just your head. Now as an adult, as these scriptures become more and more important to me, as I again read books by great people, I realize how much these "great thinkers" relied on and used the Bible. And why not? Think of the source of Biblical scripture.

The study of God's word, for the purpose of discovering God's will, is the secret discipline which has formed the greatest characters.

James W. Alexander

The book to read is not the one which thinks for you, but the one which makes you think. No book in the world equals the Bible for that.

James McCosh

Now I'd like to make a major point that has helped me and I hope will help you. These quotes, maxims, laws, sayings, or proverbs, because they are short and encapsulate wonderful truths, are not always correct. They are, after all, people's opinions. What I've tried to do in this collection is to contrast or compare them to the Bible—to use the wisdom of the Bible as our standard. You will not see here the hundreds of quotations which, in my opinion, did not pass the test. I worry that so much wrong headed advice already makes it into our everyday discourse.

Proverbs are but rules, and rules do not create character.—They prescribe conduct, but do not furnish a full and proper motive.—They are usually but half truths, and seldom contain the principle of the action they teach.

Theodore T. Munger

Reader, now I send thee, like a bee, to gather honey out of flowers and weeds; every garden is furnished with either, and so is ours. Read and meditate.

Horace Smith

An example of how damaging a wrong headed quote can be is Thomas Jefferson's statement about "a wall of separation of church and state." This was from a letter to a group of clergy attempting to gain their political support. My goodness, the damage this statement has done by being read the wrong way in the wrong hands is unbelievable. Now, people actually quote it as if it were part of our constitution.

Look at this quote, and then think of the power that so few eloquent words, written by inspiration, can have upon the intellect and the spirit.

There are powers inside of you which, if you could discover and use, would make of you everything you ever dreamed or imagined you could become.

Orison Swett Marden

Over the years I've heard and collected the quotations in this book. The best are still to be found in the Bible. Yet throughout the centuries, many great and noble men and women have weighed in on these various topics. Some of these sayings had archaic words—words we would have a tough time understanding. I've taken the literary license to bring the language forward to our time and use current words. I've tried to be careful and not change the author's true meaning. Many of these quotations were part of a larger text or speech. Time and space do not permit the full text.

I hope you enjoy these sayings. I surely enjoyed collecting them. Many have been very influential in my life and the lives of others. Please feel free to use them in your talks with your fellow workers or families. I think you'll find that the use of these quotations will uplift, inspire, edify, and, in short, improve the quality of our public discourse and private lives.

Of course there is no formula for success except, perhaps, an unconditional acceptance of life and what it brings.

Arthur Rubinstein

He who has imagination without learning has wings and no feet.

Joseph Joubert

DEVELOPING CHARACTER AND ABILITIES

Whatever the place allotted us by providence that is for us the post of honor and duty. God estimates us not by the position we are in, but by the way in which we fill it.

Tyron Edwards

Every person is responsible for all the good within the scope of his abilities, and for no more, and none can tell whose sphere is the largest.

Gail Hamilton

Habit will reconcile us to everything but change.

Caleb C. Colton

Sow an act, and you reap a habit; sow a habit, and you reap a character; sow a character, and you reap a destiny.

George Dana Boardman

To an honest mind the best perquisites of a place are the advantages it gives a man of doing good.

Joseph Addison

When we have practiced good actions awhile, they become easy; when they are easy, we take pleasure in them; when they please us, we do them frequently; and then, by frequency of act, they grow into a habit.

John Tillotson

We are all the time following the influences which will presently be our rulers; we are making our own destiny. We are choosing our habits, our associates, our traits, our homes. In time these acquire a power over us which enslaves our will, and from them we neither will nor can break loose.

Herman Lincoln Wayland

Great and good are seldom the same man.

Thomas Fuller

The chains of habit are generally too small to be felt until they are too strong to be broken.

Samuel Johnson

The end cannot justify the means for the simple and obvious reason that the means employed determine the nature of the ends produced.

Aldous Huxley

Great offices will have great talents, and God gives to every man the virtue, temper, understanding, taste, that lifts him into life, and lets him fall just in the niche he was ordained to fill.

William Cowper

We first make our habits, and then our habits make us. All habits gather, by unseen degrees, as brooks make rivers, rivers run into seas.

John Dryden

Habit, if wisely and skillfully formed, becomes truly a second nature; but unskillfully and unmethodically directed, it will be as it were the ape of nature, which imitates nothing to the life, but only clumsily and awkwardly.

Francis Bacon

Ability is a poor man's wealth.

Matthew Wren

No amount of ability is of the slightest avail without honor.

Andrew Carnegie

Aim at perfection in everything, though in most things it is unattainable.—However, they who aim at it, and persevere, will come much nearer to it than those whose laziness and despondency make them give it up as unattainable.

Philip Dormer Stanhope Chesterfield

A pint can't hold a quart—if it holds a pint it is doing all that can be expected of it.

Margaretta W. Deland

Every human soul is of infinite value, eternal, free; no human being, therefore, is so placed as not to have within his reach, in himself and others, objects adequate to infinite endeavor.

Arthur J. Balfour

It is the first rule in oratory that a man must appear such as he would persuade others to be; and that can be accomplished only by the force of his life.

Jonathan Swift

It is not the victory that makes the joy of noble hearts, but the combat.

Charles Forbes Montalembert

There is something that is much more scarce, something finer far, something rarer than ability. It is the ability to recognize ability.

Elbert Hubbard

Don't be a cynic, and bewail and bemoan.—Omit the negative propositions.—Don't waste yourself in rejection, nor bark against the bad, but chant the beauty of the good.—Set down nothing that will help somebody.

Ralph Waldo Emerson

Show me the man you honor, and I will know what kind of a man you are, for it shows me what your ideal of manhood is, and what kind of a man you long to be.

Thomas Carlyle

No man can ever be noble who thinks meanly or contemptuously of himself, and no man can ever be noble who thinks first and only of himself.

W. H. Dollinger

What a mistake to suppose that the passions are strongest in youth! The passions are not stronger, but the control over them is weaker! They are more easily excited, they are more violent and apparent; but they have less energy, less durability, less intense and concentrated power than in maturer life.

Edward George Bulwer-Lytton

Nature is upheld by antagonism.—Passions, resistance, danger, are educators. We acquire the strength we have overcome.

Ralph Waldo Emerson

There is only one real failure in life that is possible, and that is, not to be true to the best one knows.

Frederick William Farrar

Perfection is attained by slow degrees; it requires the hand of time.

Francois Marie de Voltaire

Virtue is the first title of nobility.

Jean Baptiste Moliere

7

The acorn does not become an oak in a day; the ripened scholar is not made by a single lesson; the well-trained soldier was not the raw recruit of yesterday; there are always months between the seed-time and harvest. So the path of the just is like the shining light, which shineth more and more unto the perfect day.

R.B. Nichol

Few things are impossible in themselves.—It is not so much means, as perseverance, that is wanting to bring them to a successful issue.

Francois Duc de La Rochefoucauld

The best part of health is fine disposition.

Ralph Waldo Emerson

The principles now implanted in thy bosom will grow, and one day reach maturity; and in that maturity thou wilt find thy heaven or thy hell.

David Thomas

All habits gather, by unseen degrees, as brooks make rivers, rivers run to seas.

John Dryden

Not in novelty but in habit and custom do we find the greatest pleasure.

Raymond Radiguet

Growth is the only evidence of life.

John Henry Newman

No man is truly great who is great only in his own lifetime. The test of greatness is the page of history.

William Hazlitt

Ability doth hit the mark where presumption over-shooteth and diffidence falleth short.

Nicolas Cusa

Men of talent are men for occasions. Talent is the capacity of doing anything that depends on application and industry; it is a voluntary power, while genius is involuntary.

William Hazlitt

Faith in the ability of a leader is of slight service unless it be united with faith in his justice.

General George W. Goethals

Slumber not in the tents of your fathers. The world is advancing. Advance with it.

Giuseppe Mazzini

Judge of thine improvement, not by what thou speakest or writest, but by the firmness of thy mind, and the government of thy passions and affections.

Thomas Fuller

Use your gifts faithfully, and they shall be enlarged; practice what you know, and you shall attain to higher knowledge.

Sir Edwin Arnold

The mark of the immature man is that he wants to die nobly for a cause, while the mark of the mature man is that he wants to live humble for one.

Jerome David Salinger

The history of the world is but the biography of great men.
Thomas Carlyle

An imaginary ailment is worse than a disease.

Hanan J. Ayalti

To travel hopefully is a better thing than to arrive, and the true success is to labor.

Author Unknown

Life has taught me to expect nothing, but she has to expect success to be the inevitable result of my endeavors. She taught me to seek sustenance from the endeavor itself, but to leave the result to God.

Alan Paton

If you wish success in life, make perseverance your bosom friend, experience your wise counselor, caution your elder brother, and hope your guardian genius.

Joseph Addison

Have a purpose in life, and having it, throw into your work such strength of mind and muscle as God has given you.

Thomas Carlyle

The difference between failure and success is doing a thing nearly right and doing it exactly right.

Edward C. Simmons

There is no thought in any mind, but it quickly tends to convert itself into a power, and organizes a huge instrumentality of means.

Ralph Waldo Emerson

People seldom improve when they have no other model but themselves to copy after.

Oliver Goldsmith

It is a sad thing to begin life with low conceptions of it. It may not be possible for a young man to measure life; but it is possible to say, I am resolved to put life to its noblest and best use.

Thomas T. Munger

According to Solomon, life and death are in the power of the tongue; and as Euripides truly affirmeth, every unbridled tongue in the end shall find itself unfortunate; in all that ever I observed I ever found that men's fortunes are oftener made by their tongues than by their virtues, and more men's fortunes overthrown thereby, also, than by their virtues.

Sir Walter Raleigh

The failures of life come from resting in good intentions, which are in vain unless carried out in wise action.

Charles Simmons

We want an aim that can never grow vile, and which cannot disappoint our hope. There is but one such on earth, and it is that of being like God. He who strives after union with perfect love must grow out of selfishness, and his success is secured in the omnipotent holiness of God.

Stopford A. Brooke

What are the aims which are at the same time duties?—they are the perfecting of ourselves, and the happiness of others.

Immanuel Kant

Goodness consists not in the outward things we do, but in the inward thing we are.—To be good is a great thing.

Edwin Hubbell Chapin

Life shrinks or expands in proportion to one's courage.

Anaïs Nin

Heaven never helps the man who will not act.

Sophocles

Infinite toil would not enable you to sweep away a mist; but by ascending a little you may often look over it altogether. So it is with our moral improvement; we wrestle fiercely with a vicious habit, which would have no hold upon us if we ascended into a higher moral atmosphere.

Sir Arthur Helps

Nothing great was ever achieved without enthusiasm.

Ralph Waldo Emerson

Remember you have not a sinew whose law of strength is not action; not a faculty of body, mind, or soul, whose law of improvement is not energy.

E. B. Hall

Of all virtues and dignities of the mind, goodness is the greatest, being the character of the Deity; and without it, man is a busy, mischievous, wretched thing.

Francis Bacon

A good name lost is seldom regained.—When character is gone, all is gone, and one of the richest jewels of life is lost forever.

Joel Hawes

God helps them that help themselves.

Old Proverb

Haste is not always speed. We must learn to work and wait. This is like God, who perfects his works through beautiful gradations.

Author Unknown

He is good that does good to others. If he suffers for the good he does, he is better still; and if he suffers from them to whom he did good, he has arrived to that height of goodness that nothing but an increase of his sufferings can add to it; if it proves his death, his virtue is at its summit; it is heroism complete.

Jean de la Bruyére

The higher we rise, the more isolated we become; all elevations are cold.

Marquis Stanislas Jean de Boufflers

In great attempts it is glorious even to fail.

Dionysius Longinus

It seems to me it is only noble to be good.—Kind hearts are more than coronets.

Lord Alfred Tennyson

To be good, we must do good; and by doing good we take a sure means of being good, as the use and exercise of the muscles increase their power.

Tyron Edwards

Subtlety may deceive you; integrity never will.

Oliver Cromwell

Most men are more capable of great actions than of good ones.

Charles de Secondat Montesquieu

All cruelty springs from hard-heartedness and weakness.

Lucius Annaeus Seneca

Be not merely good; be good for something.
Henry David Thoreau

Cruelty, like every other vice, requires no motive outside of itself; it only requires opportunity.

George Eliot

It is a maxim with me, that no man was ever written out of a reputation but by himself.

Richard Bentley

Never despair; but if you do, work on in despair.

Edmund Burke

Those who honestly mean to be true contradict themselves more rarely than those who try to be consistent.

Oliver Wendell Holmes

LOVE, AGE, AND FAMILIES

Old age is wise for itself, but not for the community.—It is wise in declining new enterprises, for it has not the power or the time to execute them; wise in shrinking from difficulty, for it has not the strength to overcome it; wise in avoiding danger, for it lacks the faculty of ready and swift action by which dangers are parried and converted into advantages.—But this is not wisdom for mankind at large, by whom new enterprises must be undertaken, dangers met, and difficulties surmounted.

William Cullen Bryant

Every one desires to live long, but no one would be old.

Jonathan Swift

As I approve of a youth that has something of the old man in him, so I am no less pleased with an old man that has something of the youth. He that follows this rule, may be old in body, but can never be so in mind.

Marcus Tullius Cicero

The more people have studied different methods of bringing up children the more they have come to the conclusion that what good mothers and fathers instinctively feel like doing for their babies is the best after all.

Benjamin Spock

Children need models rather than critics.

Joseph Joubert

You are worried about seeing him spend his early years in doing nothing. What! Is it nothing to be happy? Nothing to skip, play, and run around all day long? Never in his life will he be so busy again.

Jean Jacques Rousseau

No better heritage can a father bequeath to his children than a good name; nor is there in a family any richer heirloom than the memory of a noble ancestor.

James Hamilton

There are few successful adults who were not at first successful children.

Alexander Chase

Whatever you would have your children become, strive to exhibit in your own lives and conversation.

Lydia H. Sigourney

The child is father of the man.

William Wordsworth

I love these little people; and it is not a slight thing, when they, who are so fresh from God, love us.

Charles Dickens

Children are God's apostles, sent forth, day by day, to preach of love, and hope and peace.

James Russell Lowell

To withhold from a child some knowledge apportioned to his understanding of the world's sorrows and wrongs is to cheat him of his kinship with humanity.

Agnes Repplier

Childhood shows the man, as morning shows the day.

John Milton

Every man is his own ancestor, and every man is his own heir. He devises his own future and he inherits his own past.

Frederick Henry Hedge

Faith in God hallows and confirms the union between parents and children, and subjects and rulers.—Infidelity relaxes every band, and nullifies every blessing.

Johann Pestalozzi

The future destiny of the child is always the work of the mother.

Napoleon Bonaparte

A torn jacket is soon mended; but hard words bruise the heart of a child.
Henry Wadsworth Longfellow

It is always safe to follow the religious belief that our mother taught us; there never was a mother yet who taught her child to be an infidel.

Henry Wheeler Shaw

There is in all this cold and hollow world no fount of deep, strong, deathless love, save that within a mother's heart.

Felicia Hemans

We never know the love of the parent till we become parents ourselves. When we first bend over the cradle of our own child, God throws back the temple door, and reveals to us the sacredness and mystery of a father's and mother's love to ourselves.—And in later years, when they have gone from us, there is always a certain sorrow, that we cannot tell them we have found it out.—One of the deepest experiences of a noble nature in reference to the loved ones that have passed beyond this world, is the thought of what he might have been to them, and done for them, if he had known, while they were living, what he has learned since they died.

Henry Ward Beecher

Children, look in those eyes, listen to that dear voice, notice the feeling of even a single touch that is bestowed upon you by that gentle hand! Make much of it while yet you have that most precious of all good gifts, a loving mother. Read the unfathomable love of those eyes; the kind of anxiety of that tone and look, however slight your pain. In after life you may have friends, fond, dear friends, but never will you have again the inexpressible love and gentleness lavished upon you, which none but a mother bestows.

Thomas Babington Macaulay

If we would amend the world we should mend ourselves and teach our children to be not what we are but what they should be.

William Penn

Love is a canvas furnished by Nature and embroidered by imagination.

Francois Marie de Voltaire

When Eve was brought unto Adam, he became filled with the Holy Spirit, and gave her the most sanctified, the most glorious of appellations. He called her Eve, that is to say, the Mother of All. He did not style her wife, but simply mother,—mother of all living creatures. In this consists the glory and the most precious ornament of woman.

Martin Luther

Nature's loving proxy, the watchful mother.

Edward George Bulwer-Lytton

"What is wanting," said Napoleon one day to Madame Campan, "in order that the youth of France be well educated?" "Good mothers," was the reply. The Emperor was most forcibly struck with this answer. "Here," said he, "is a system in one word."

John S. C. Abbott

The mother in her office holds the key of the soul; and she it is who stamps the coin of character, and makes the being who would be a savage but for her gentle cares, a Christian man! Then crown her queen of the world.

Old Play

All that I am, or hope to be, I owe to my angel mother.

Abraham Lincoln

The cure for all the ills and wrongs, the cares, the sorrows, and the crimes of humanity, all lie in that one word "love." It is the divine vitality that everywhere produces and restores life. To each and every one of us, it gives the power of working miracles if we will.

Lydia M. Child

The family is the association established by nature for the supply of man's everyday wants.

Aristotle

It is the general rule, that all superior men inherit the elements of superiority from their mothers.

Jules Michelet

Let us leave the beautiful women to men with no imagination.

Marcel Proust

Observe how soon, and to what a degree, a mother's influence begins to operate! Her first ministration for her infant is to enter, as it were, the valley of the shadow of death, and win its life at the peril of her own! How different must an affection thus founded be from all others!

Lydia H. Sigourney

A father may turn his back on his child; brothers and sisters may become inveterate enemies; husbands may desert their wives, and wives their husbands. But a mother's love endures through all; in good repute, in bad repute, in the face of the world's condemnation, a mother still loves on, and still hopes that her child may turn from his evil ways, and repent; still she remembers the infant smiles that once filled her bosom with rapture, the merry laugh, the joyful shout of his childhood, the opening promise of his youth; and she can never be brought to think him unworthy.

Washington Irving

Oh, wondrous power! How little understood, entrusted to the mother's mind alone, to fashion genius, form the soul for good, inspire a West, or train a Washington.

Sarah J. Hale

An ounce of mother is worth a pound of clergy.
Spanish Proverb

Let France have good mothers, and she will have good sons.

Napoleon Bonaparte

A mother's love is indeed the golden link that binds youth to age; and he is still but a child, however time may have furrowed his cheek, or silvered his brow, who can yet recall, with a softened heart, the fond devotion, or the gentle chidings, of the best friend that God ever gives us.

Christian Nestell Bovee

It is generally admitted, and very frequently proved, that virtue and genius, and all the natural good qualities which men possess, are derived from their mothers.

Theodore Edward Hooke

Love, it has been said, flows downward. The love of parents for their children has always been far more powerful than that of children for their parents; and who among the sons of men ever loved God with a thousandth part of the love which God has manifested to us?

August W. Hare

No language can express the power and beauty and heroism and majesty of a mother's love. It shrinks not where man cowers, and grows stronger where man faints, and over the wastes of worldly fortune sends the radiance of its quenchless fidelity like a star in heaven.

Edwin Hubbell Chapin

Even He that died for us upon the cross, in the last hour, in the unutterable agony of death, was mindful of his mother, as if to teach us that this holy love should be our last worldly thought,—the last point of earth from which the soul should take its flight for heaven.

Henry Wadsworth Longfellow

I would desire for a friend the son who never resisted the tears of his mother.

Jean Charles Lacretelle

The voice of parents is the voice of gods, for to their children they are heaven's lieutenants.

William Shakespeare

Honor thy parents, those that gave thee birth, and watched in tenderness thine earliest days, and trained thee up in youth, and loved in all. Honor, obey, and love them; it shall fill their souls with holy joy, and shall bring down God's richest blessing on thee; and in days to come, thy children, if they're given, shall honor thee, and fill thy life with peace.

Tryon Edwards

The sacred books of the ancient Persians say: If you would be holy, instruct your children, because all the good acts they perform will be imputed to you.

Charles de Secondat Montesquieu

The father and mother of an unnoticed family, who in their seclusion awaken the mind of one child to the idea and love of goodness, who awaken in him a strength of will to repel temptations, and who send him out prepared to profit by the conflicts of life, surpass in influence a Napoleon breaking the world to his sway.

William Ellery Channing

Our home joys are the most delightful earth affords, and the joy of parents in their children is the most holy joy of humanity. It makes their hearts pure and good, it lifts men up to their Father in heaven.

Johann Pestalozzi

If you would reform the world from its errors and vices, begin by enlisting the mothers.

Charles Simmons

God could not be everywhere, and therefore he made mothers.

Jewish Saying

If there be one thing pure, where all beside is sullied, and that can endure when all else passes away—if aught surpassing human deed, or word, or thought, it is a mother's love.

Spadara

Memory, wit, fancy, acuteness, cannot grow young again in old age; but the heart can.

Jean Paul Richter

Parents must give good example and reverent deportment in the face of their children. And all those instances of charity which endear each other—sweetness of conversation, affability, frequent admonition—all significations of love and tenderness, care and watchfulness, must be expressed toward children; that they may look upon their parents as their friends and patrons, their defense and sanctuary, their treasure and their guide.

Author Unknown

Certain it is that there is no kind of affection so purely angelic as the love of a father to a daughter. He beholds her both with and without regard to her sex.—In love to our wives, there is desire; to our sons, there is ambition; but in that to our daughters there is something which there are no words to express.

Joseph Addison

Civilization varies with the family, and the family with civilization.—Its highest and most complete realization is found where enlightened Christianity prevails; where woman is exalted to her true and lofty place as equal with the man; where husband and wife are one in honor, influence, and affection, and where children are a common bond of care and love.—This is the idea of a perfect family.

William Aikman

We speak of educating our children. Do we know that our children also educate us?
Lydia H. Sigourney

There is not a man or woman, however poor they may be, but have it in their power, by the grace of God, to leave behind them the grandest thing on earth, character; and their children might rise up after them and thank God that their mother was a pious woman, or their father a pious man.

Norman Macleod

Every house where love abides and friendship is a guest is surely home, and home, sweet home; for there the heart can rest.

Henry Van Dyke

If we're not foolish young, we're foolish old.

Geoffrey Chaucer

"Many of our cares," says Scott, "are but a morbid way of looking at our privileges."—We let our blessings get mouldy, and then call them curses.

Henry Ward Beecher

Of all the paths leading to a woman's love, pity is the straightest.

Francis Beaumont

The heart has reasons that reason does not understand.

Jacques Bénigne Bossuet

We are shaped and fashioned by what we love.

Johann Wolfgang von Goethe

The generous heart should scorn a pleasure which gives others pain.

James Thomson

In a full heart there is room for everything, and in an empty heart there is room for nothing.

Antonio Porchia

We know too much and feel too little. At least, we feel too little of those creative emotions from which a good life springs.

Bertrand Russell

If a man loves a woman for her beauty, does he love her? No; for the small-pox, which destroys her beauty without killing her, causes his love to cease. And if any one loves me for my judgment or my memory, does he really love me? No; for I can lose these qualities without ceasing to be.

Blaise Pascal

Until I loved I was alone.

Caroline Norton

It is a beautiful necessity of our nature to love something.

Douglas Jerrold

There is a kind of sympathy in souls that fits them for each other; and we may be assured when we see two persons engaged in the warmths of a mutual affection, that there are certain qualities in both their minds which bear a resemblance to one another.

Sir Richard Steele

Nothing more excites to all that is noble and generous, than virtuous love.

Henry Home

Absence in love is like water upon fire; a little quickens, but much extinguishes it.

Hannah More

The heart of him who truly loves is a paradise on earth; he has God in himself, for God is love.

Abbé Hugo Félicité de Lamennais

Love is the most terrible, and also the most generous of the passions; it is the only one that includes in its dreams the happiness of someone else.

Jean Baptiste Alphonse

The plainest man that can convince a woman that he is really in love with her, has done more to make her in love with him than the handsomest man, if he can produce no such conviction. For the love of woman is a shoot, not a seed, and flourishes most vigorously only when ingrafted on that love which is touted in the breast of another.

Caleb C. Colton

All true love is grounded on esteem.

George Villiers Buckingham

The passions are the winds that fill the sails of the vessel.—They sink it at times; but without them it would be impossible to make way.—Many things that are dangerous here below, are still necessary.

Francois Marie de Voltaire

It is better to have loved and lost, than not to love at all.

Lord Alfred Tennyson

Love which is only an episode in the life of man, is the entire history of woman's life.

Madam de Staël

A man loved by a beautiful and virtuous woman, carries with him a talisman that renders him invulnerable; every one feels that such a one's life has a higher value than that of others.

Amantine Lucile Aurore Dudevant

Mutual love, the crown of all our bliss.

John Milton

Love is a thing to be learned. It is a difficult, complex maintenance of individual integrity throughout the incalculable processes of inter-human polarity.

David H. Lawrence

A man may be a miser of his wealth; he may tie up his talent in a napkin; he may hug himself in his reputation; but he is always generous in his love. Love cannot stay at home; a man cannot keep it to himself. Like light, it is constantly traveling. A man must spend it, must give it away.

Alexander Macleod

We speak of hope; but is not hope only a more gentle name for fear?

Letitia Elizabeth Landon

It is the duty of men to love even those who injure them.

Marcus Antoninus

A woman cannot love a man she feels to be her inferior; love without veneration and enthusiasm is only friendship.

Amantine Lucile Aurore Dudevant

Love sought is good, but given unsought is better.
William Shakespeare

Love is the purification of the heart from self; it strengthens and ennobles the character, gives a higher motive and a nobler aim to every action of life, and makes both man and woman strong, noble, and courageous; and the power to love truly and devotedly is the noblest gift with which a human being can be endowed; but it is a sacred fire that must not be burned to idols.

Maria Jane Jewsbury

Love is strongest in pursuit; friendship in possession.

Ralph Waldo Emerson

All loves should be simply stepping stones to the love of God. So it was with me; and blessed be his name for his great goodness and mercy.

Plato

The soul of woman lives in love.

Lydia H. Sigourney

There is a passion of reverence, almost of pity, mingling with the love of an honest man for a pure girl, which makes it the most exquisite, perhaps, of all human sentiments.

Lucas Malet

Husband and wife who have fought the world side by side, who have made common stock of joy or sorrow, and become aged together, are not unfrequently found curiously alike in personal appearance, in pitch and tone of voice, just as twin pebbles on the beach, exposed to the same tidal influences, are each other's alter ego.

Alexander Smith

Base men, being in love, have then a nobility in their natures, more than is native to them.

William Shakespeare

It is astonishing how little one feels poverty when one loves.

Edward George Bulwer-Lytton

We attract hearts by the qualities we display: we retain them by the qualities we possess.

Jean Baptiste Antoine Suard

It seems to me that the coming of love is like the coming of spring—the date is not to be reckoned by the calendar. It may be slow and gradual; it may be quick and sudden. But in the morning, when we wake and recognize a change in the world without, verdure on the trees, blossoms on the yard, warmth in the sunshine, music in the air, we say spring has come.

Edward George Bulwer-Lytton

A man reserves his greatest and deepest love not for the woman in whose company he finds himself electrified and enkindled but for that one in whose company he may feel tenderly drowsy.

George Jean Nathan

Love is an image of God, and not a lifeless image, but the living essence of the divine nature which beams full of all goodness.

Martin Luther

Where there is room in the heart there is always room in the house.

Sir Thomas Moore

It is possible that a man can be so changed by love as hardly to be recognized as the same person.

Terence

We never know how much one loves till we know how much he is willing to endure and suffer for us; and it is the suffering element that measures love.—The characters that are great, must, of necessity, be characters that shall be willing, patient, and strong to endure for others.—To hold our nature in the willing service of another is the divine idea of manhood, of the human character.

Henry Ward Beecher

It is the very essence of love, of nobleness, of greatness, to be willing to suffer for the good of others.

Spence

Love needs new leaves every summer of life, as much as your elm-tree, and new branches to grow broader and wider, and new flowers to cover the ground.

Harriet Beecher Stowe

Passion is the great mover and spring of the soul: when men's passions are strongest, they may have great and noble effects; but they are then also apt to fall into the greatest miscarriages.

Thomas Sprat

The future of society is in the hands of the mothers. If the world was lost through woman, she alone can save it.

Louis de Beaufort

If there is anything better than to be loved, it is loving.

Anonymous

Where there is the most love to God, there will be there the truest and most enlarged philanthropy.

Robert Southey

Frequent intercourse and intimate connection between two persons, make them so alike, that not only their dispositions are moulded like to each other, but their very faces and tones of voice contract a similarity.

John Caspar Lavater

Love, and you shall be loved.—All love is mathematically just, as much as the two sides of an algebraic equation.

Ralph Waldo Emerson

The babe at first feeds upon the mother's bosom, but is always on her heart.

Henry Ward Beecher

Love is the hardest lesson in Christianity; but for that reason, it should be most our care to learn it.

William Penn

The current of tenderness widens as it proceeds; two men imperceptibly find their hearts filled with good nature for each other, when they were at first only in pursuit of mirth and relaxation.

Oliver Goldsmith

The less tenderness a man has in his nature the more he requires of others.

Ibn Rahel

The ways of the heart, like the ways of providence, are mysterious.

Henry Ware

Next to love, sympathy is the divinest passion of the human heart.

Edmund Burke

We love a girl for very different things than understanding. We love her for her beauty, her youth, her mirth, her confidingness, her character, with its faults, caprices, and God knows what other in-expressible charms; but we do not love her understanding. Her mind we esteem if it is brilliant, and it may greatly elevate her in our opinion; nay, more, it may enchain us when we already love. But her understanding is not that which awakens and inflames our passions.

Johann Wolfgang von Goethe

Love one human being purely and warmly, and you will love all.—The heart in this heaven, like the sun in its course, sees nothing, from the dewdrop to the ocean, but a mirror which it brightens, and warms, and fills.

Jean Paul Richter

PATRIOTISM AND GOVERNMENT

Men are qualified for civil liberty in exact proportion to their disposition to put chains upon their own appetites; in proportion as their love of justice is above their rapacity; in proportion as their soundness and sobriety of understanding is above their vanity and presumption; in proportion as they are more disposed to listen to the counsels of the wise and good, in preference to the flattery of knaves. Society cannot exist unless a controlling power upon the will and appetite is placed somewhere; and the less of it there is within, the more there must be of it without. It is ordained in the eternal constitution of things that men of intemperate habits cannot be free. Their passions forge their fetters.

Edmund Burke

These lands are ours. No one has a right to remove us, because we were the first owners. The Great Spirit above has appointed this place for our use.

Tecumseh

The making of an American begins at that point where he himself rejects all other ties, and any other history, and himself adopts the vesture of his adopted land.

James Baldwin

Here in America we are descended in spirit from revolutionists and rebels—men and women who dare to dissent from accepted doctrine.

Dwight D. Eisenhower

If I were asked...to what the singular prosperity and growing strength of [Americans] ought mainly to be attributed, I should reply: to the superiority of their women.

Alexis Charles Henry de Tocqueville

If we mean to support the liberty and independence which have cost us so much blood and treasure to establish, we must drive far away the demon of party spirit and local reproach.

George Washington

Freedom of speech and freedom of action are meaningless without freedom to think. And there is no freedom of thought without doubt.

Bergen Evans

We hold these truths to be self-evident, that all men are created equal; that they are endowed by their Creator with inalienable rights; and that among these are life, liberty, and the pursuit of happiness.

Thomas Jefferson

I call that mind free which jealously guards its intellectual rights and powers, which calls no man master, which does not content itself with a passive or hereditary faith, [and] receives new truth as an angel from Heaven.

William Ellery Channing

Freedom is the will to be responsible to ourselves.

Friedrich W. Nietzsche

There is danger from all men. The only maxim of a free government ought to be to trust no man living with power to endanger the public liberty.

John Quincy Adams

Give me the liberty to know, to think, to believe, and to utter freely, according to conscience, above all other liberties.

John Milton

The political parties that I would call great, are those which cling more to principles than to consequences; to general, and not to special cases; to ideas, and not to men.—Such parties are usually distinguished by a nobler character, more generous passions, more genuine convictions, and a more bold and open conduct than others.

Alexis Charles Henry de Tocqueville

Is life so dear, or peace so sweet as to be purchased at the price of chains and slavery?—Forbid it, Almighty God!—I know not what course others may take, but, as for me, give me liberty or give me death.

Patrick Henry

There are two freedoms, the false where one is free to do what he likes, and the true where he is free to do what he ought.
Charles Kingsley

Liberty and union, one and inseparable, now and forever.

Daniel Webster

Bad men cannot make good citizens. It is impossible that a nation of infidels or idolaters should be a nation of free-men. It is when a people forget God that tyrants forge their chains. A vitiated state of morals, a corrupted public conscience, is incompatible with freedom.

Anonymous

No free government, or the blessings of liberty can be preserved to any people but by a firm adherence to justice, moderation, temperance, frugality, and virtue, and by a frequent recurrence to fundamental principles.

Patrick Henry

Perfect conformity to the will of God is the sole sovereign and complete liberty.

Jean Henri Merle D'Aubigné

No man can always do just as he chooses until he always chooses to do God's will; and that is heaven. There is no liberty in wrong-doing.—It chains and fetters its victim as surely as effect follows cause.

Joseph Cook

The greatest glory of a free-born people, is to transmit that freedom to their children.

William Havard

It is foolish to strive with what we cannot avoid; we are born subjects, and to obey God is perfect liberty; he that does this, shall be free, safe and quiet; all his actions shall succeed to his wishes.

Lucius Annaeus Seneca

A country cannot subsist well without liberty, nor liberty without virtue.

Jean Jacques Rousseau

True liberty consists in the privilege of enjoying our own rights, not in the destruction of the rights of others.

George Pinckard

Liberty will not descend to a people; a people must raise themselves to liberty; it is a blessing that must be earned before it can be enjoyed.

Caleb C. Colton

It is impossible to enslave, mentally or socially, a Bible-reading people. The principles of the Bible are the groundwork of human freedom.

Horace Greeley

Power, to its last particle, is duty.

John Foster

A Bible and a newspaper in every house, a good school in every district,—all studied and appreciated as they merit,—are the principal support of virtue, morality, and civil liberty.

Benjamin Franklin

A nation may lose its liberties in a day, and not miss them in a century.

Charles de Secondat Montesquieu

The human race is in the best condition when it has the greatest degree of liberty.

Dante Alighieri

Nothing can bring you peace but yourself; nothing can bring you peace but the triumph of principles.

Ralph Waldo Emerson

The principle, that "God alone is Lord of the conscience," has done more to give the mind power, and to strike off its chains, then any principle of mere secular policy in the most perfect "Bill of Rights."

Gardiner Spring

No peace was ever won from fate by subterfuge or agreement; no peace is ever in store for any of us, but that which we shall win by victory over shame or sin,—victory over the sin that oppresses, as well as over that which corrupts.

John Ruskin

Love of country is one of the loftiest virtues; and so treason against it has been considered among the most damning sins.

Emery Alexander Storrs

Peace is such a precious jewel that I would give anything for it but truth.

Matthew Henry

Five great enemies to peace inhabit with us: avarice, ambition, envy, anger, and pride. If those enemies were to be banished, we should enjoy perpetual peace.

Petrarch

There is no liberty to men who know not how to govern themselves.

Henry Ward Beecher

A day, an hour, of virtuous liberty is worth a whole eternity of bondage.

Joseph Addison

If we have not peace within ourselves, it is in vain to seek it from outward sources.

Francois Duc de La Rochefoucauld

To be prepared for war is one of the most effectual means of preserving the peace.

George Washington

The age of virtuous politics is past, and we are deep in that of cold pretense.—Patriots are grown too shrewd to be sincere, and we too wise to trust them.

William Cowper

Let our object be our country, our whole country, and nothing but our country. And, by the blessing of God, may that country itself become a vast and splendid monument, not of oppression and terror, but of wisdom, of peace, and of liberty, upon which the world may gaze with admiration forever.

Daniel Webster

The worst thing in this world, next to anarchy, is government.

Henry Ward Beecher

Interwoven is the love of liberty with every ligament of the heart.

George Washington

National enthusiasm is the great nursery of genius.

Henry Theodore Tuckerman

There can be no affinity nearer than our country.

Plato

No matter what theory of the origin of government you adopt, if you follow it out to its legitimate conclusions it will bring you face to face with the moral law.

Henry Van Dyke

When men put their trust in God and in knowledge, the government of the majority is, in the end, the government of the wise and good.

William Spalding

No government ought to exist for the purpose of checking the prosperity of its people or to allow such a principle in its policy.

Edmund Burke

Government owes its birth to the necessity of preventing and repressing the injuries which associated individuals have to fear from one another.—It is the sentinel who watches, in order that the common laborer be not disturbed.

Abbé Rayna

The culminating point of administration is to know well how much power, great or small, we ought to use in all circumstances.

Charles de Secondat Montesquieu

Millions for defense, but not one cent for tribute.

Charles Coatesworth Pinckney

The actual achievement of democracy is that it gives a tolerably good time to the underdog. Or, at least, it tries; and it is, I think, for this reason that most of us accept it as our political creed.

Sir James Jeans

The world is governed by three things—wisdom, authority, and appearance. Wisdom for thoughtful people, authority for rough people, and appearances for the great mass of superficial people who can look only at the outside.

Author Unknown

The great political controversy of the ages has reached its end in the recognition of the individual.—The socialistic party would again sink the individual in the government, and make it possible for the government to perpetuate itself and become absolute.

Francis Cassette Monfort

No government is respectable which is not just.—Without unspotted purity of public faith, without sacred public principle, fidelity, and honor, no mere forms of government, no machinery of laws, can give dignity to political society.

Daniel Webster

A politician thinks of the next election; a statesman of the next generation.—A politician looks for the success of his party; a statesman for that of his country.—The statesman wishes to steer, while the politician is satisfied to drift.

James F. Clarke

The punishment suffered by the wise who refuse to take part in the government, is to live under the government of bad men.

Plato

45

The aggregate happiness of society, which is best promoted by the practice of a virtuous policy, is, or ought to be, the end of all government.

George Washington

When any of the four pillars of government, religion, justice, counsel, and treasure, are mainly shaken or weakened, men had need to pray for fair weather.

Francis Bacon

The less government we have the better—the fewer laws and the less confided power. The antidote to this abuse of formal government is the influence of private character, the growth of the individual.

Ralph Waldo Emerson

A republican government is a hundred points weaker than one that is autocratic; but in this one point it is the strongest that ever existed—it has educated a race of men that are men.

Henry Ward Beecher

Taxing is an easy business. Any projector can contrive new impositions; any bungler can add to the old; but is it altogether wise to have no other bounds to your impositions than the patience of those who are to bear them?

Edmund Burke

The test of any government is the extent to which it increases the good in the people.

Aristotle

It is a very easy thing to devise good laws; the difficulty is to make them effective. The great mistake is that of looking upon men as virtuous, or thinking that they can be made so by laws; and consequently the greatest art of a politician is to render vices serviceable to the cause of virtue.

Lord Bolingbroke

Taxation without representation is injustice and oppression. It brought on the American Revolution, and gave birth to a free and mighty nation.

Author Unknown

The surest way of governing, both in a private family and a kingdom, is for the husband and the prince sometimes to drop their prerogatives.

Thomas Hughes

All good government must begin in the home.—It is useless to make good laws for bad people.—Public sentiment is more than law.

Hugh R. Haweis

Perfect freedom is necessary to the health and vigor of commerce, as it is to the health and vigor of citizenship.

Patrick Henry

The true strength of rulers and empires lies not in armies or emotions, but in the belief of men that they are inflexibly open and truthful and legal. As soon as a government departs from that standard it ceases to be anything more than "the gang in possession," and its days are numbered.

H. G. Wells

Society is well governed when the people obey the magistrates, and the magistrates obey the laws.

Solon

The riches we impart are the only wealth we shall always retain.

Matthew Henry

That is the most perfect government under which a wrong to the humblest is an affront to all.

Solon

When civilizations fail, it is almost always man who has failed—not in his body, not in his fundamental equipment and capacities, but in his will, spirit, and mental habits.

Philip Lee Ralph

Knowledge of [another] culture should sharpen our ability to scrutinize more steadily, to appreciate more lovingly, our own.

Margaret Mead

As a hawk flieth not high with one wing, even so a man reacheth not to excellence with one tongue.

Roger Ascham

In the commerce of speech use only coin of gold and silver.

Joseph Joubert

There is no tracing the connection of ancient nations but by language; therefore I am always sorry when any language is lost, for languages are the pedigree of nations.

Samuel Johnson

I am wonderfully delighted to see a body of men thriving in their own fortunes, and at the same time promoting the public stock; or, in other words, raising estates for their own families by bringing into their country whatever is wanting, and carrying out of it whatever is superfluous.

Joseph Addison

The form of government is unimportant—the spirit everything.

General Von Schmidt

The best protection of a nation is its men; towns and cities cannot have a surer defense than the prowess and virtue of their inhabitants.

Francois Rabelais

Commerce tends to wear off those prejudices which maintain destruction and animosity between nations.—It softens and polishes the manners of men.—It unites them by one of the strongest of all ties—the desire of supplying their mutual wants.—It disposes them to peace by establishing in every state an order of citizens bound by their interest to be the guardians of public tranquillity.

Frederick William Robertson

It is written in God's word, and in all the history of the race, that nations, if they live at all, live not by felicity of position, or soil, or climate, and not by abundance of material good, but by the living word of the living God.—The commandments of God are the bread of life for the nations.

Roswell Dwight Hitchcock

Territory is but the body of a nation.—The people who inhabit its hills and valleys are its soul, its spirit, its life.

James A. Garfield

The test of every religious, political, or education system is the man that it forms.

Henri Frederic Amiel

The great hope of society is in individual character.

William Ellery Channing

A man who is ignorant of foreign languages is ignorant of his own.

Johann Wolfgang von Goethe

No nation can be destroyed while it possesses a good home life.

Josiah Gilbert Holland

Blessed are the young, for they shall inherit the national debt.

Herbert Hoover

49

There is an opinion that parties in free countries are useful checks upon the administration of the government, and serve to keep alive the spirit of liberty. This, within certain limits, is probably true. But in governments of a popular character, and purely elective, it is a spirit not to be encouraged. From their natural tendency, there will always be enough of that spirit for every salutary purpose. And there being constant danger of excess, the effort ought to be, by force of public opinion, to mitigate and assuage it. A fire not to be quenched, it demands a uniform vigilance to prevent it bursting into a flame, lest, instead of warming, it should consume.

George Washington

Kings ought to shear, not skin, their sheep.

Robert Herrick

A state to prosper, must be built on foundations of a moral character, and this character is the principal element of its strength, and the only guaranty of its permanence and prosperity.

Jabez Curry

The private and personal blessings we enjoy, the blessings of immunity, safeguard, liberty, and integrity, deserve the thanksgiving of a whole life.

Jeremy Taylor

When the press is the echo of sages and reformers, it works well; when it is the echo of turbulent cynics, it merely feeds political excitement.

Alphonse de Lamartine

It may almost be held that the hope of commercial gain has done nearly as much for the cause of truth, as even the love of truth itself.

Christian Nestell Bovee

There can be no high civility without a deep morality.

Ralph Waldo Emerson

The character of a people, like the character of a person, should not be measured by its worst, but rather by its best; and, reckoned by that rule and by that standard, Israel's rank is high.

David H. Greer

Let us with caution indulge the supposition that morality can be maintained without religion. Reason and experience both forbid us to expect that national morality can prevail in exclusion of religious principle.

George Washington

The true grandeur of nations is in those qualities which constitute the true greatness of the individual.

Charles Sumner

We want the spirit of America to be efficient; we want American character to be efficient; we want American character to display itself in what I may, perhaps, be allowed to call spiritual efficiency—clear disinterested thinking and fearless action along the right lines of thought.

Thomas Woodrow Wilson

It is not money, nor is it mere intellect, that governs the world; it is moral character, and intellect associated with moral excellence.

Theodore Dwight Woolsey

We should never create by law what can be accomplished by morality.

Charles de Secondat
Montesquieu

Capitalism inevitably and by virtue of the very logic of its civilization creates, educates and subsidizes a vested interest in social unrest.

Joseph Schumpeter

From the beginning of our history the country has been afflicted with compromise. It is by compromise that human rights have been abandoned. I insist that this shall cease. The country needs repose after all it's trials; it deserves repose. And repose can only be found in everlasting principles.

Charles Sumner

As for the just and noble idea that nations, as well as individuals, are parts of one wondrous whole, it has hardly passed the lips or pen of any but religious men and poets.—It is the one great principle of the greatest religion which has ever nourished the morals of mankind.

Harriet Martineau

The law is a sort of hocus-pocus science that smiles in your face while it picks your pocket; and the glorious uncertainty of it is of more use to the professors than the justice of it.

Charles Macklin

A nation's character is the sum of its splendid deeds; they constitute one common patrimony, the nation's inheritance. They awe foreign powers, they arouse and animate our own people.

Henry Clay

When the state is most corrupt, then the laws are most multiplied.

Tactitus

A natural law is a process, not a power; it is a method of operation, not an operator. A natural law, without God behind it, is no more than a glove without a hand in it.

Joseph Cook

If religious books are not widely circulated among the masses in this country, and the people do not become religious, I do not know what is to become of us as a nation. And the thought is one to cause solemn reflection on the part of every patriot and Christian. If truth be not diffused, error will be; if God and his word are not known and received, the devil and his works will gain the ascendancy; if the evangelical volume does not reach every hamlet, the pages of a corrupt and licentious literature will; if the power of the gospel is not felt through the length and breadth of the land, anarchy and misrule, degradation and misery, corruption and darkness, will reign without mitigation or end.

Daniel Webster

National progress is the sum of individual industry, energy, and uprightness, as national decay is of individual idleness, selfishness, and vice.

Samuel Smiles

When with true American enthusiasm we recall the story of our war for independence and rejoice in the indomitable courage and fortitude of our revolutionary heroes, we should not fail to remember how well the Jews of America performed their part in the struggle.

Grover Cleveland

As the laws are above magistrates, so are the magistrates above the people; and it may truly be said, that the magistrate is a speaking law, and the law a silent magistrate.

Marcus Tullius Cicero

These written laws are just like spiders' webs; the small and feeble may be caught and entangled in them, but the rich and mighty force through and despise them.

Anacharsis

Nobility should be elective, not hereditary.
Johann Georg Zimmerman

53

A knowledge of the laws of our country is a highly useful, and I had almost said essential part of liberal and polite education.

Anonymous

Responsibilities gravitate to the person who can shoulder them; power flows to the man who knows how.

Elbert Hubbard

We are not to lead events, but follow them.

Epictetus

It is better to have a lion at the head of an army of sheep, than a sheep at the head of an army of lions.

Daniel DeFoe

Communism possesses a language which every people can understand.—Its elements are hunger, envy, and death.

Heinrich Heine

A statesman, we are told, should follow public opinion; doubtless as a coachman follows his horses, having firm hold on the reins, and guiding them.

Julius Charles Hare

The true grandeur of nations is in those qualities which constitute the true greatness of the individual.

Charles Sumner

ACQUIREMENT

Never live in hope or expectation while your arms are folded. God helps those that help themselves. Providence smiles on those who put their shoulders to the wheel that propels to wealth and happiness. It is only the constant exertion and working of our sensitive, intellectual, moral, and physical machinery that keeps us from rusting, and so becoming useless.

Charles Simmons

Since the generality of persons act from impulse much more than from principle, men are neither so good nor so bad as we are apt to think them.

August W. Hare

What we truly and earnestly aspire to be, that in some sense we are.—The mere aspiration, by changing the frame and spirit of the mind, for the moment realizes itself.

Anna Jameson

Some men give up their designs when they have almost reached the goal; while others, on the contrary, obtain a victory by exerting, at the last moment, more vigorous efforts than before.

Polybius

Nothing is so powerful as an idea when its hour has come.

Victor Hugo

That which we acquire with most difficulty we retain the longest; as those who have earned a fortune are commonly more careful of it than those by whom it may have been inherited.

Caleb C. Colton

It is very rare to find ground which produces nothing.—If it is not covered with flowers, fruit trees, and grains, it produces briars and pines.—It is the same with man; if he is not virtuous, he becomes vicious.

Jean de la Bruyére

One that desires to excel should endeavor it in those things that are in themselves most excellent.

Epictetus

If a man empties his purse into his head, no one can take it from him.—An investment in knowledge always pays the best interest.

Benjamin Franklin

Every noble acquisition is attended with its risks; he who fears to encounter the one must not expect to obtain the other.

Pietro Metastasio

An unjust acquisition is like a barbed arrow which must be drawn backward with horrible anguish, or else will be your destruction.

Jeremy Taylor

Whatever the mind can conceive and believe, men can achieve.

Andrew Carnegie

Men are often capable of greater things than they perform.—The are sent into the world with bills of credit, and seldom draw to their full extent.

Horace Walpole

He who always seeks more light, the more he finds, and finds more the more he seeks, is one of the few happy mortals who take and give in every point of time. The time and ebb of giving and receiving is the sum of human happiness, which he alone enjoys who always wishes to acquire new knowledge, and always finds it.

John Caspar Lavater

If you don't know what you want, you won't recognize it when you get it.

Anonymous

Those who attain to any excellence commonly spend life in some one single pursuit, for excellence is not often gained upon easier terms.

Samuel Johnson

The man who is fond of complaining, likes to remain amid the objects of his vexation.—It is at the moment that he declares them insupportable that he will most strongly revolt against every means proposed for his deliverance.—This is what suits him.—He asks nothing better than to sigh over his position and to remain in it.

Francois Pierre Guizot

I will not be as those who spend the day in complaining of headache, and the night in drinking the wine that gives it.

Johann Wolfgang von Goethe

That is true cultivation which gives us sympathy with every form of human life, and enables us to work most successfully for its advancement. Refinement that carries us away from our fellow-men is not God's refinement.

Henry Ward Beecher

The man who succeeds above his fellows is the one who, early in life, clearly discerns his object, and towards that object habitually directs his powers. Even genius itself is but fine observation strengthened by fixity of purpose. Every man who observes vigilantly and resolves steadfastly grows uncon-sciously into genius.

Edward George Bulwer-Lytton

The usual fortune of complaint is to excite contempt more than pity.

Samuel Johnson

It is not in mortals to command success, but we will do more, we will deserve it.

Joseph Addison

Whatever expands the affections, or enlarges the sphere of our sympathies—whatever makes us feel our relation to the universe and all that it inherits in time and in eternity, and to the great and beneficent cause of all, must unquestionably refine our nature, and elevate us in the scale of being.

William Ellery Channing

All earthly delights are sweeter in expectation than in enjoyment; but all spiritual pleasures more in fruition than in expectation.

Owen Feltham

Not what men do worthily, but what they do successfully, is what history makes haste to record.

Henry Ward Beecher

The richest genius, like the most fertile soil, when uncultivated, shoots up into the rankest weeds; and instead of vines and olives for the pleasure and use of man, produces to its slothful owner the most abundant crop of poisons.

David Hume

The true way to gain much, is never to desire to gain too much.—He is not rich that possesses much, but he that covets no more; and he is not poor that enjoys little, but he that wants too much.

Francis Beaumont

THINKING BIG
AND
WORKING HARD

Industry need not wish, and he that lives upon hopes will die fasting. There are no gains without pains. He that hath a trade hath an estate, and he that hath a calling hath an office of profit and honor; but then the trade must be worked at, and the calling followed, or neither the estate nor the office will enable us to pay our taxes. If we are industrious, we shall never starve; for, at the workingman's house hunger looks in, but dares not enter. Nor will the bailiff or the constable enter, for industry pays debts, while idleness and neglect increase them.

Benjamin Franklin

It is not for man to rest in absolute contentment.—He is born to hopes and aspirations as the sparks fly upward, unless he has brutified his nature and quenched the spirit of immortality which is his portion.

Robert Southey

It seems to me we can never give up longing and wishing while we are thoroughly alive. There are certain things we feel to be beautiful and good, and we must hunger after them.

George Eliot

God has never ceased to be the one true aim of all right human aspirations.

Alexander R. Vinet

Too many wish to be happy before becoming wise.

Madame Necker

Live only today, and you ruin tomorrow.

Charles Simmons

If I had wished to raise up a race of statesmen higher than politicians, animated not by greed or selfishness, by policy or party, I would familiarize the boys of the land with the characters of the Bible.

John Hall

Trust men and they will be true to you; treat them greatly and they will show themselves great.

Ralph Waldo Emerson

To form a correct judgment concerning the tendency of any doctrine we should look rather at the forms it bears in the disciples, than in the teacher, for he only made it; they are made by it.

Julius Charles Hare

Ah, but a man's reach should exceed his grasp, or what's heaven for?

Robert Browning

One often passes from love to ambition but rarely returns from ambition to love.

Francois Duc de La Rochefoucauld

If you have great talents, industry will improve them; if moderate abilities, industry will supply their deficiencies. Nothing is denied to well-directed labor; nothing is ever to be attained without it.

Sir Joshua Reynolds

There is always hope in a man who actually and earnestly works.—In idleness alone is there perpetual despair.

Thomas Carlyle

Great opportunities come to all, but many do not know they have met them.—The only preparation to take advantage of them is simple fidelity to what each day brings.

Albert Elijah Dunning

It is better to wear out than to rust out.

Richard Cumberland

One loses all the time which he might employ to better purpose.

Jean Jacques Rousseau

Ambition is the germ from which all growth of nobleness proceeds.

Thomas Dunn English

They can conquer who believe they can.
John Dryden

The celebrated Galen said that employment was nature's physician.—It is indeed so important to happiness that laziness is justly considered the parent of misery.

Caleb C. Colton

Industry keeps the body healthy, the mind clear, the heart whole, and the purse full.

Charles Simmons

Every industrious man, in every lawful calling, is a useful man.—And one principle reason why men are so often useless is that they neglect their own profession or calling, and divide and shift their attention among a multiplicity of objects and pursuits.

Nathaniel Emmons

An hour's industry will do more to produce cheerfulness, suppress evil humors, and retrieve one's affairs, than a month's moaning.—It sweetens enjoyment, and seasons our attainments with a delightful relish.

Isaac Barrow

A man who gives his children habits of industry provides for them better than by giving them a fortune.

Richard Whately

Industry hath annexed thereto the fairest fruits and the richest rewards.

Isaac Barrow

The chiefest action for a man of spirit is never to be out of action; the soul was never put into the body to stand still.

John Webster

To have ideas is to gather flowers; to think, is to weave them into garlands.

Madame Swetchine

There is a tide in the affairs of men, which, taken at the flood, leads on to fortune; omitted, all the voyage of their life is bound in shallows and in miseries; and we must take the current when it serves, or lose our ventures.

William Shakespeare

For truth and duty it is ever the fitting time; who waits until circumstances completely favor his undertaking, will never accomplish anything.

Martin Luther

Every one has a fair turn to be as great as he pleases.

Jeremy Collier

A healthful idea is usually original to more than one discoverer.—Great ideas come when the world needs them.— They surround the world's ignorance and press for admission.

Austin Phelps

I can not commend to a business house any artificial plan for making men producers—any scheme for driving them into business-building. You must lead them through their self-interest.

Charles H. Steinway

If you want to succeed in the world you must make your own opportunities as you go on. The man who waits for some seventh wave to toss him on dry land will find that the seventh wave is a long time a coming. You can commit no greater folly than to sit by the roadside until some one comes along and invites you to ride with him to wealth or influence.

John B. Gough

The secret of success in life, is for a man to be ready for his opportunity when it comes.

Benjamin Disraeli

What no beautician would ever tell a woman is that the secret to being beautiful is thinking the right thoughts.

WNBC radio

Mark this well, ye proud men of action! Ye are, after all, nothing but unconscious instruments of the men of thought.

Heinrich Heine

All that a man does outwardly is but the expression and completion of his inward thought. To work effectively, he must think clearly; to act nobly, he must think nobly. Intellectual force is a principle element of the soul's life, and should be proposed by every man as the principal end of his being.

William Ellery Channing

Cowardice asks, "Is it safe?" Expediency asks, "Is it politic?" Vanity asks, "Is it popular?" But Conscience asks, "Is it right?"

William Morley Pushon

The greatest events of an age are its best thoughts. Thought finds its way into action.

Boise

Many ideas grow better when transplanted into another mind than in the one where they sprung up. That which was a weed in one becomes a flower in the other, and a flower again dwindles down to a mere weed by the same change. Healthy growths may become poisonous by falling upon the wrong mental soil, and what seemed a nightshade in one mind unfolds as a morning-glory in the other.

Oliver Wendell Holmes

A soul occupied with great ideas best performs small duties.

Harriet Martineau

An idea, like a ghost, according to the common notion of ghosts, must be spoken to a little before it will explain itself.

Charles Dickens

Our opportunities to do good are our talents.

Cotton Mather

Our ideas, like orange-plants, spread out in proportion to the size of the box which imprisons the roots.

Edward George Bulwer-Lytton

Let us unite contemplation with action.—In the harmony of the two, lies the perfection of character.—They are not contradictory and incompatible, but mutually helpful to each other.—Contemplation will strengthen for action, and action sends us back to contemplation, and thus the inner and outer life will be harmoniously developed.

Alexander L. R. Foote

Everyone must see and feel that bad thoughts quickly ripen into bad actions; and that, if the latter only are forbidden, and the former left free, all morality will soon be at an end.

Beilby Porteus

Unless a man has trained himself for his chance, the chance will only make him ridiculous. A great occasion is worth to a man exactly what his antecedents have enabled him to make of it.

William Mathews

Ideas control the world.
James A. Garfield

Who makes quick use of the moment, is a genius of prudence.

John Caspar Lavater

There are no times in life when opportunity, the chance to be and do, gathers so richly about the soul as when it has to suffer. Then everything depends on whether the man turns to the lower or the higher helps. If he resorts to mere expedients and tricks the opportunity is lost. He comes out no richer nor greater; nay, he comes out harder, poorer, smaller for his pain. But if he turns to God, the hour of suffering is the turning hour of his life.

Phillips Brooks

A wise man will make more opportunities than he finds.

Francis Bacon

One couldn't carry on life comfortably without a little blindness to the fact that everything has been said better than we can put it ourselves.

George Eliot

It is better to create than to be learned; creating is the true essence of life

Berthold G. Niebuhr

Every human being is intended to have a character of his own; to be what no other is, and to do what no other can do.

William Ellery Channing

They who have light in themselves, will not revolve as satellites.

Anonymous

Originality is nothing but judicious imitation.—The most original writers borrowed one from another. The instruction we find in books is like fire. We fetch it from our neighbor's, kindle it at home, communicate it to others, and it becomes the property of all.

Francois Marie de Voltaire

One of the best uses of originality is to say common things in an uncommon way.

Author Unknown

Thought convinces; feeling persuades.—If imagination furnishes the fact with wings, feeling is the great stout muscle which plies them, and lifts him from the ground.—Thought sees beauty; emotion feels it.

Theodore Parker

We satisfied ourselves, the other day, that there was no real ill in life except severe bodily pain; everything else is the child of the imagination, and depends on our thoughts.—All other ills find a remedy either from time, or moderation, or strength of mind.

Madame de Sevigne

It is almost impossible for any one who reads much, and reflects a good deal, to be able, on every occasion, to determine whether a thought was another's or his own.—I have several times quoted sentences out of my own writings, in aid of my own arguments, in conversation, thinking that I was supporting them by some better authority.

Lawrence Sterne

Boredom is a sickness, the cure for which is work; pleasure is only a palliative.

Le Duc de Lévis

The creative person is both more primitive and more cultivated, more destructive, a lot madder and a lot saner, than the average person.

Frank Barron

Imagination disposes of everything; it creates beauty, justice, and happiness, which are everything in this world.

Blaise Pascal

Originality is simply a pair of fresh eyes.

Thomas Wentworth Higginson

Someone praising a man for his fool-hardy bravery, Cato, the elder, said, "There is a wide difference between true courage and a mere contempt of life."

Plutarch

The creative person is not well brought up, he is ill-mannered [and] thumbs his nose at respectability.

Elsa Triolet

An ill-humored man, is, almost of course, a selfish man, unhappy in himself, and disagreeable to others.—His chief pleasure seems to be, to be displeased, if not with himself, yet with all about him.

Author Unknown

Imagination rules the world.

Napoleon Bonaparte

Imagination, where it is truly creative, is a faculty, not a quality; its seat is in the higher reason, and it is efficient only as the servant of the will.—Imagination, as too often understood, is mere fantasy—the image-making power, common to all who have the gift of dreams.

James Russell Lowell

The soul without imagination is what an observatory would be without a telescope.

Henry Ward Beecher

Nature often enshrines gallant and noble hearts in weak bosoms; oftenest, God bless here, in a woman's breast.

Charles Dickens

Some critics are like chimney-sweepers; they put out the fire below, and frighten the swallows from their nests above; they scrape a long time in the chimney, cover themselves with soot, and bring nothing away but a bag of cinders, and then sing out from the top of the house, as if they had built it.

Henry Wadsworth Longfellow

Imagination is the eye of the soul.

Joseph Joubert

A true knight is fuller of bravery in the midst, than in the beginning of danger.

Sir Philip Sidney

At the bottom of not a little of the bravery that appears in the world, there lurks a miserable cowardice. Men will face power and steel because they have not the courage to face public opinion.

Edwin Hubbell Chapin

Prosperity is no just scale; adversity is the only balance to weigh friends.

Plutarch

True bravery is shown by performing without witnesses what one might be capable of doing before all the world.

Francois Duc de La Rochefoucauld

Genuine good taste consists in saying much in few words, in choosing among our thoughts, in having order and arrangement in what we say, and in speaking with composure.

Bishop Francis de S. Fenelon

Man must be arched and buttressed from within, else the temple wavers to the dust.

Marcus Aurelius

The bravery founded on hope of recompense, fear of punishment, experience of success, on rage, or on ignorance of danger, is but common bravery, and does not deserve the name.— True bravery proposes a just end; measures the dangers, and meets the result with calmness and unyielding decision.

Francois de La Noue

All brave men love; for he only is brave who has affections to fight for, whether in the daily battle of life, or in physical contests.

Nathaniel Hawthorne

Opinions are stronger than armies.—If they are founded in truth and justice, they will, in the end, prevail against the bayonets of infantry, the fire of artillery, and the charges of cavalry.

Lord Palmerston

As it is the characteristic of great wits to say much in few words, so it is of small wits to talk much and say nothing.

Francois Duc de La Rochefoucauld

Applause waits on success; the fickle multitude, like the light straw that floats along the stream, glides with the current skill, and follows fortune.

Benjamin Franklin

Necessity is the mother of invention.

George Farquhar

Brevity is the soul of wit.
William Shakespeare

Grumblers are commonly an idle set.—Having no deposition to work themselves, they spend their time in whining and complaining both about their own affairs and those of their neighbors.

Author Unknown

76

Just as you are pleased at finding faults, you are displeased at finding perfections.

John Caspar Lavater

Let your words be few, especially when your betters, or strangers, or men of more experience, or understanding, are in the place, for in so doing you do yourself at once two great mischiefs: first, you betray, and discover your own weakness and folly; and next, you rob yourself of that opportunity which you might otherwise have to gain wisdom and experience, by hearing those that you silence by your impertinent talking.

Sir Matthew Hale

Men judge us by the success of our efforts. God looks at the efforts themselves.

Charlotte Elizabeth

Murmur at nothing. If our ills are reparable, it is ungrateful; if remediless, it is vain. A Christian builds his fortune on a better foundation than stoicism; he is pleased with every thing that happens, because he knows it could not happen if it did not please God; and that which pleases God must be best.

Herman Lincoln Wayland

He who murmurs against his condition, does not understand it; but he who accepts of it in peace, will soon learn to comprehend it. What one has experienced and learned in this respect, is always a stage he has made on his way to heaven.

Author Unknown

Beware of prejudices. They are like rats, and men's minds are like traps; prejudices get in easily, but it is doubtful if they ever get out.

Author Unknown

Those who complain most are most to be complained of.
Matthew Henry

Acts are nothing except as they are fruits of a state, except as they indicate what the man is; words are nothing except as they express a mind or purpose.

John Frederick Dennison Maurice

The taxes are indeed very heavy, and if those laid by government were the only ones we had to pay, we might more easily discharge them; but we have many others, and much more grievous to some of us. We are taxed twice as much by idleness, three times as much by our pride, and four times as much by our folly; and from these taxes the commissioners cannot ease or deliver us by allowing an abatement.

Benjamin Franklin

We may be as good as we please, if we please to be good.

Isaac Barrow

It is not a lucky word, this same "impossible;" no good comes of those who have it so often in their mouth.

Thomas Carlyle

Reasoning against a prejudice is like fighting against a shadow; it exhausts the reasoner, without visibly affecting the prejudice. Argument cannot do the work of instruction any more than blows can take the place of sunlight.

Arundell Charles Saint John Mildmay

Impossible is a word only to be found in the dictionary of fools.

Napoleon Bonaparte

The great obstacle to progress is prejudice.

Christian Nestell Bovee

A superior man is modest in his speech, but exceeds in his actions.

Confucius

Every year of my life I grow more convinced that it is wisest and best to fix our attention on the beautiful and the good, and dwell as little as possible on the evil and the false.

Richard Cecil

When it comes to changes, people like only those they make themselves.

French Proverb

It will generally be found that those who sneer habitually at human nature, and affect to despise it, are among its worst and least pleasant samples.

Charles Dickens

As plants take hold, not for the sake of staying, but only that they may climb higher, so it is with men.—By every part of our nature we clasp things above us, one after another, not for the sake of remaining where we take hold, but that we may go higher.

Henry Ward Beecher

Among the other excellencies of man, this is one, that he can form the image of perfection much beyond what he has experience of in himself, and is not limited in his conception of wisdom and virtue.

David Hume

When we destroy an old prejudice we have need of a new virtue.

Madam de Staël

Shame on those hearts of stone, that cannot melt in soft adoption of another's sorrow!

Aaron Hill

Modesty is a shining light; it prepares the mind to receive knowledge, and the heart for truth.

Francois Pierre Guizot

The faculty of imagination is the great spring of human activity, and the principle source of human improvement. As it delights in presenting to the mind scenes and characters more perfect than those which we are acquainted with, it prevents us from ever being completely satisfied with our present condition, or with our past attainments, and engages us continually in the pursuit of some untried enjoyment, or of some ideal excellence. Destroy this faculty, and the condition of man will become as stationary as that of the brutes.

Dugald Stewart

Character is the result of two things: Mental attitude and the way we spend our time.

Elbert Hubbard

There is so much good in the worst of us, and so much bad in the best of us, that it behooves all of us not to talk about the rest of us.

Robert Louis

Fortune befriends the bold.

John Dryden

I hold a doctrine, to which I owe not much, indeed, but all the little I ever had, namely that with ordinary talent and extraordinary perseverance, all things are attainable.

Sir Thomas Fowell Buxton

He who is lord of himself, and exists upon his own resources, is a noble but a rare being.

Samuel E. Brydges

It is only imperfection that complains of what is imperfect.—The more perfect we are, the more gentle and quiet we become toward the defects of others.

Bishop Francis de S. Fenelon

Experience has convinced me that there is a thousand times more goodness, wisdom, and love in the world than men imagine.

Gehles

Conscience is not law.—No.—God has made and reason recognizes the law, and conscience is placed within us to prompt to the right, and warn against the wrong. A disciplined conscience is a man's best friend.—It may not be his most amiable, but it is his most faithful monitor.

Austin Phelps

Look upon every day as the whole of life, not merely as a section; and enjoy and improve the present without wishing, through haste, to rush on to another.

Jean Paul Richter

It is better to be nobly remembered, than nobly born.

John Ruskin

Man is, properly speaking, based upon hope; he has no other possession but hope; this world of his is emphatically the place of hope.

Thomas Carlyle

It is worth a thousand pounds a year to have the habit of looking on the bright side of things.
Samuel Johnson

81

Let any man examine his thoughts, and he will find them ever occupied with the past or the future. We scarcely think at all of the present; or if we do, it is only to borrow the light which it gives for regulating the future. The present is never our object; the past and present we use as means; the future only is our end. Thus, we never live, we only hope to live.

Blaise Pascal

Enjoy the blessings of this day, if God sends them; and the evils bear patiently and sweetly; for only this day is ours; we are dead to yesterday, and not born tomorrow.

Jeremy Taylor

A tender conscience is an inestimable blessing; that is, a conscience not only quick to discern what is evil, but instantly to shun it, as the eyelid closes itself against the mote.

Nehemiah Adams

Seek not the favor of the multitude; it is seldom got by honest and lawful means. But seek the testimony of the few: and number not voices, but weigh them.

Immanuel Kant

THE SPIRITUAL SIDE OF LIFE

As to all that we have and are, we are but stewards of the Most High God. On all our possessions, on our time, and talents, and influence, and property, he has written, "Occupy for me till I shall come." To obey his instructions and serve him faithfully is the true test of obedience and discipleship.

Charles Simmons

They produce, in proportion to their numbers, an unusually large number of able and successful men as any one may prove by recounting the eminent Jews of the last seventy years.

James Bryce

The character of a people, like the character of a person, should not be measured by its worst, but rather by its best; and, reckoned by that rule and by that standard, Israel's rank is high.

David H. Greer

In defiance of all the torture, the might, and the malice of the world, the liberal man will ever be rich; for God's providence is his estate, God's wisdom and power his defense, God's love and favor his reward, and God's word his security.

Isaac Barrow

The three great apostles of practical atheism, that make converts without persecuting, and retain them without preaching, are wealth, health and power.

Caleb C. Colton

The Christian ideal has not been tried and found wanting. It has been found difficult and left untried.

Gilbert K. Chesterton

One day a man was asked if there were any true atheists. Do you think, he replied, that there are any true Christians?

Denis Diderot

I wish [Christianity] were more productive of good works. I mean real good works...not holy-day keeping, sermon-hearing, or making long prayers filled with flatteries and compliments despised by wise men and much less capable of pleasing the Deity.

Benjamin Franklin

The way to begin a Christian life is not to study theology. Piety before theology. Right living will produce right thinking. Theologies are well in their place, but repentance and love must come before all other experiences.

Henry Ward Beecher

If there is one part of the Christian message that people have rejected with incomparable obstinacy, it is faith in the equal worth of all souls and races before the Father who is in heaven.

Francois Mauriac

If religion does nothing for your temper it has done nothing for your soul.

Robert Clayton

Here is what Christian living entails: wishing in all things whatever God wishes, desiring His glory, seeking nothing for oneself, either now or in the hereafter.

Martin Luther

If the world is ever conquered for Christ, it will be by every one doing their own work, filling their own sphere, holding their own post, and saying to Jesus, Lord, what wilt thou have me to do.

Thomas Guthrie

There is a beauty in the name appropriated by the Saxon nations to the Deity, unequalled except by his most venerated Hebrew appellation. They called him "God," which is literally "The Good." The same word thus signifying the Deity and His most enduring quality.

Charles Tennyson Turner

Neutral men are the devil's allies.

Edwin Hubbell Chapin

God's thoughts, his will, his love, his judgments are all man's home. To think his thoughts, to choose his will, to love his loves, to judge his judgments, and thus to know that he is in us, is to be at home.

George MacDonald

The study of God's word, for the purpose of discovering God's will, is the secret discipline which has formed the greatest characters.

James W. Alexander

The man who consecrates his hours by vigorous effort, and an honest aim, at once he draws and sting of life and death; he walks with nature; and her paths are peace.

Edward Young

Speak, move, act in peace, as if you were in prayer. In truth, this is prayer.

Bishop Francis de S. Fenelon

The best theology is rather a divine life than a divine knowledge.

Jeremy Taylor

The root of the matter...is love, Christian love, or compassion. If you feel this, you have a motive for existence, a guide for action, a reason for courage [and] for intellectual honesty.

Bertrand Russell

The very word "God" suggests care, kindness, goodness; and the idea of God in his infinity, is infinite care, infinite kindness, infinite goodness.—We give God the name of good: it is only by shortening it that it becomes God.

Henry Ward Beecher

At the foot of every page in the annals of nations may be written, "God reigns." Events as they pass away proclaim their original; and if you will but listen reverently, you may hear the receding centuries, as they roll into the dim distances of departed time, perpetually chanting "Te Deum Laudamus," with all the choral voices of the countless congregations of the age.

George Bancroft

God should be the object of all our desires, the end of all our actions, the principle of all our affections, and the governing power of our whole souls.

Jean Baptiste Massillon

God is great, and therefore he will be sought: he is good, and therefore he will be found.

Author Unknown

If in the day of sorrow we own God's presence in the cloud, we shall find him also in the pillar of fire, brightening and cheering our way as the night comes on.

Author Unknown

A wise physician is a John Baptist, who recognizes that his only mission is to prepare the way for a greater than himself.

Arthur S. Hardy

A foe to God was never a true friend to man.

Edward Young

In all his dispensations God is at work for our good.—In prosperity he tries our gratitude; in mediocrity, our contentment; in misfortune, our submission; in darkness, our faith; under temptation, our steadfastness, and at all times, our obedience and trust in him.

Author Unknown

How often we look upon God as our last and feeblest resource! We go to him because we have nowhere else to go. And then we learn that the storms of life have driven us, not upon the rocks, but into the desired haven.

George MacDonald

Health, beauty, vigor, riches, and all the other things called goods, operate equally as evils to the vicious and unjust, as they do as benefits to the just.

Plato

Amid all the war and contest and variety of human opinion, you will find one consenting conviction in every land, that there is one God, the king and father of all.

Tyrius Maximus

How many observe Christ's birthday! How few his precepts! O! 'tis easier to keep holidays than commandments.

Benjamin Franklin

How far that little candle throws his beams! So shines a good deed in a naughty world.

William Shakespeare

The world we inhabit must have had an origin; that origin must have consisted in a cause; that cause must have been intelligent; that intelligence must have been supreme; and that supreme, which always was and is supreme, we know by the name of God.

Author Unknown

In all thine actions think that God sees thee, and in all his actions labor to see him.—That will make thee fear him, and this will move thee to love him.—The fear of God is the beginning of knowledge, and the knowledge of God is the perfection of love.

Francis Quarles

In the heraldry of heaven goodness precedes greatness, and so on earth it is more powerful.—The lowly and lovely may often do more good in their limited sphere than the gifted.

Bishop George Horne

Sorrow is the handmaid of God, not of Satan. She would lead us, as she did the Psalmist, to say, "Who will show us any good?" that after having said this we may also say with him, "Lord, lift thou the light of thy countenance upon us."

Arthur S. Hardy

Bearing up against temptations and prevailing over them is the very thing wherein the whole life of religion consists. It is the trial which God puts upon us in this world, by which we are to make evidence of our love and obedience to him, and of our fitness to be made members of his kingdom.

Samuel Clarke

Wherever souls are being tried and ripened, in whatever commonplace and homely way, there God is hewing out the pillars for His temple.

Phillips Brooks

The beloved of the Almighty are the rich who have the humility of the poor, and the poor who have the magnanimity of the rich.

Saadi

His daily prayer, far better understood in acts than in words, was simply doing good.

John Greenleaf Whittier

Sorrows gather around great souls as storms do around mountains; but, like them, they break the storm and purify the air of the plain beneath them.

Jean Paul Richter

Covetous men are fools, miserable wretches, buzzards, madmen, who live by themselves, in perpetual slavery, fear, suspicion, sorrow, discontent, with more of gall than honey in their enjoyments; who are rather possessed by their money than possessors of it, bound 'prentices to their property, mean slaves and drudges to their substance.

Richard E. Burton

God never gave a man a thing to do, concerning which it were irreverent to ponder how the Son of God would have done it.

George MacDonald

Every step toward Christ kills a doubt. Every thought, word, and deed for Him carries you away from discouragement.

Theodore Ledyard Cuyler

As the flower is before the fruit, so is faith before good works.

Richard Whately

Nothing can make a man truly great but being truly good and partaking of God's holiness.

Matthew Henry

The happiest, sweetest, tenderest homes are not those where there has been no sorrow, but those which have been overshadowed with grief, and where Christ's comfort was accepted. The very memory of the sorrow is a gentle benediction that broods ever over the household, like the silence that comes after prayer. There is a blessing sent from God in every burden of sorrow.

John R. Miller

The longer I live, the more convincing proofs I see of this truth, that God governs in the affairs of man; and if a sparrow cannot fall to the ground without his notice, is it probable that an empire can rise without his aid?

Benjamin Franklin

The ablest men in all walks of modern life are men of faith. Most of them have much more faith than they themselves realize.

Bruce Barton

Providence is a greater mystery than revelation. The state of the world is more humiliating to our reason than the doctrines of the Gospel. A reflecting Christian sees more to excite his astonishment, and to exercise his faith, in the state of things between Temple Bar and St. Paul's, than in what he reads from Genesis to Revelation.

Richard Cecil

It is one of my favorite thoughts, that God manifests himself to mankind in all wise, good, humble, generous, great and magnanimous men.

John Caspar Lavater

In his life, Christ is an example, showing us how to live; in his death, he is a sacrifice, satisfying for our sins; in his resurrection, a conqueror; in his ascension, a king; in his intercession, a high priest.

Martin Luther

Let us learn upon earth, those things which can prepare us for heaven.

Saint Jerome

Blessings ever wait on virtuous deeds, and though late, a sure reward succeeds.

William Congreve

Duties are ours; events are God's.—This removes an infinite burden from the shoulders of a miserable, tempted, dying creature.—On this consideration only can he securely lay down his head and close his eyes.

Richard Cecil

Great thoughts alone change men and women. By the great thoughts of Jesus, men and women, for some two thousand years, have been changed from folly to the ways of wisdom, from baseness to wholesomeness, from cruelty to mercifulness, from sin to righteousness.

Herrick Johnson

True piety hath in it nothing weak, nothing sad, nothing constrained. It enlarges the heart; it is simple, free, and attractive.

Bishop Francis de S. Fenelon

Faith in the ability of a leader is of slight service unless it be united with faith in his justice.

General George W. Goethals

Faith and works are like the light and heat of a candle; they cannot be separated.

Author Unknown

None but a theology that came out of eternity can carry you and me safely to and through eternity.

Theodore Ledyard Cuyler

Man owes not only his services, but himself to God.

William Secker

I believe Plato and Socrates. I believe in Jesus Christ.

Samuel Taylor Coleridge

I do not doubt but that genuine piety is the spring of peace of mind; it enables us to bear the sorrows of life, and lessens the pangs of death; the same cannot be said of irreligion.

Jean de la Bruyére

I count all that part of my life lost which I spent not in communion with God, or in doing good.

John Donne

Piety is a silver chain uniting heaven and earth, temporal and spiritual, God and man together.

Nicolas Caussin

We are surrounded by motives to piety and devotion, if we would but mind them. The poor are designed to excite our liberality: the miserable, our pity; the sick, our assistance; the ignorant, our instruction; those that are fallen our helping hand. In those who are vain, we see the vanity of the world; in those who are wicked, our own frailty. When we see good men rewarded, it confirms our hope; and when evil men are punished, it excites our fear.

Daniel Wilson

The greatest concept I've ever heard is personal account-ability to an almighty Creator.
William E. Gladstone

Prayer covers the whole of a man's life. There is no thought, feeling, yearning, or desire, however low, trifling, or vulgar we may deem it, which, if it affects our real interest or happiness, we may not lay before God and be sure of his sympathy. His nature is such that our often coming does not tire him. The whole burden of the whole life of every man may be rolled on to God and not weary him, though it has wearied the man.

Henry Ward Beecher

The soul, of origin divine, God's glorious image, freed from clay, in heaven's eternal sphere shall shine, a star of day! The sun is but a spark of fire, a transient meteor in the sky; the soul immortal, as its sire, shall never die.

Robert Montgomery

The intellect of man sits visibly enthroned upon his forehead and in his eye, and the heart of man is written upon his countenance. But the soul reveals itself in the voice only, as God revealed Himself to the prophet of old in the still small voice, and in the voice from the burning bush.

Henry Wadsworth Longfellow

A mind full of piety and knowledge is always rich; it is a bank that never fails; it yields a perpetual dividend of happiness.

Author Unknown

Every temptation is great or small according as the man is.

George Eliot

All I have seen teaches me to trust the Creator for all I have not seen.

Ralph Waldo Emerson

The human soul is like a bird that is born in a cage. Nothing can deprive it of its nature longings, or obliterate the mysterious remembrance of its heritage.

Epes Sargent

It is one thing to be tempted, another thing to fall.

William Shakespeare

Every moment of resistance to temptation is a victory.

Frederick William Faber

To realize God's presence is one of the sovereign remedies against temptation.

Bishop Francis de S. Fenelon

Prayer is a sincere, sensible, affectionate pouring out of the soul to God, through Christ, in the strength and assistance of the Spirit, for such things as God has promised.

John Bunyan

Prayer is not overcoming God's reluctance; it is laying hold of His highest willingness.

Richard C. Trench

Prayer is not eloquence, but earnestness; not the definition of helplessness, but the feeling of it; not figures of speech, but earnestness of soul.

Hannah More

Whatsoever we beg of God, let us also work for it.

Jeremy Taylor

The prayer that begins with trustfulness, and passes on into waiting, will always end in thankfulness, triumph, and praise.

Alexander Maclaren

Faith always implies the disbelief of a lesser fact in favor of a greater.
Oliver Wendell Holmes

I believe I should have been swept away by the flood of infidelity, if it had not been for one thing: the remembrance of the time when my sainted mother used to make me kneel by her side, taking my little hands in hers, and caused me to repeat the Lord's Prayer.

John Randolph

Any heart turned God-ward, feels more joy in one short hour of prayer, than e'er was raised by all the feasts on earth since its foundation.

Gamaliel Bailey

I have been driven many times to my knees by the overwhelming conviction that I had nowhere else to go. My own wisdom, and that of all about me, seemed insufficient for the day.

Abraham Lincoln

Holy, humble, penitent, believing, earnest, persevering prayer is never lost; it always prevails to the accomplishment of the thing sought, or that with which the suppliant will be better satisfied in the end, according to the superior wisdom of his heavenly father, in which he trusts.

Robert Kelley Weeks

God's way of answering the Christian's prayer for more patience, experience, hope, and love, often is to put him into the furnace of affliction.

Richard Cecil

The soul would have no rainbow had the eyes no tears.
John Vance Cheney

I have lived to thank God that all my prayers have not been answered.

Jean Ingelow

The greatest prayer is patience.

Gautama Buddha

Prayer is as much the instinct of my nature as a Christian, as it is a duty enjoined by the command of God. It is my language of worship, as a man; of dependence, as a creature; of submission, as a subject; of confession, as a sinner; of thankfulness, as a recipient of mercies; of supplication, as a needy being.

Tryon Edwards

He who runs from God in the morning will scarcely find Him the rest of the day.

John Bunyan

Trouble and perplexity drive me to prayer, and prayer drives away perplexity and trouble.

Philip Melanchthon

The end of our prayers is often gained by an answer very different from what we expect. "Lord, what wilt thou have me to do?" was the question of Paul; and a large part of the answer was, "I will show him how great [the] things he must suffer."

Tryon Edwards

Open thy heart to God, if he be there, the outspread world will be thy book of prayer.

Friedrich August Tholuck

The Christian will find his parentheses for prayer even in the busiest hours of life.

Richard Cecil

We should pray with as much earnestness as those who expect everything from God; and should act with as much energy as those who expect everything from themselves.

Caleb C. Colton

God is better served in resisting a temptation to evil than in many formal prayers.

William Penn

I have been benefited by praying for others; for by making an errand to God for them I have gotten something for myself.

Samuel Rutherford

So weak is man, so ignorant and blind, that did not God sometimes withhold in mercy what we ask, we should be ruined at our own request.

Hannah More

Each time thou wishest to decide upon performing some enterprise, raise the eyes to heaven, pray to God to bless thy project; if thou canst make that prayer, accomplish thy work.

Leopold Schefer

All the duties of religion are eminently solemn and venerable in the eyes of children. But none will so strongly prove the sincerity of the parent; none so powerfully awaken the reverence of the child; none so happily recommend the instruction he receives, as family devotions, particularly those in which petitions for the children occupy a distinguished place.

Timothy Dwight

Guard well thy thoughts; our thoughts are heard in Heaven.

Edward Young

Thy word is a lamp unto my feet, and a light unto my path.

Psalm 119:105

God is infinitely great in himself; we should recognize it in humble adoration: always good; we should acknowledge it by grateful thanksgiving: we have constant need of his blessings; it becomes us to ask them at his hand.

Tryon Edwards

In the morning, prayer is the key that opens to us the treasure of God's mercies and blessings; in the evening, it is the key that attends us under his protection and safeguard.

Author Unknown

It is as natural and reasonable for a dependent creature to apply to its Creator for what it needs, as for a child to solicit the aid of a parent who is believed to have the disposition and ability to bestow what it needs.

Archibald Alexander

No man can hinder our private addresses to God; every man can build a chapel in his breast, himself the priest, his heart the sacrifice, and the earth he treads on, the altar.

Jeremy Taylor

If you would have God hear you when you pray, you must hear him when he speaks.—He stops his ears against the prayers of those who stop their ears against his laws.

Author Unknown

Never was faithful prayer lost.— Some prayers have a longer voyage than others, but then they return with their richer lading at last, so that the praying soul is a gainer by waiting for an answer.

William Gurnall

Practice in life whatever you pray for, and God will give it to you more abundantly.

Edward B. Pusey

When we pray for any virtue, we should cultivate the virtue as well as pray for it; the form of your prayer should be the rule of your life; every petition to God is a precept to man. Look not, therefore, upon your prayers as a method of good and salvation only, but as a perpetual admonition of duty. By what we require of God we see what he requires of us.

Jeremy Taylor

All the distinctive features and superiority of our republican institutions are derived from the teachings of the Scripture.

Edward Everett

God looks not at the oratory of your prayers, how elegant they may be; nor at the geometry of your prayers, how long they may be; nor at the arithmetic of your prayers, how many they may be; nor at logic of your prayers, how methodical they may be; but the sincerity of them he looks at.

Thomas Brooks

The greater thy business is, by so much the more thou hast need to pray for God's good-speed and blessing upon it, seeing it is certain nothing can prosper without his blessing. The time spent in prayer never hinders, but furthers and prospers a man's journey and business: therefore, though thy haste be never so much, or thy business never so great, yet go not about it, nor out of thy doors, till though hast prayed.

James Roosevelt

A good man's prayers will from the deepest dungeon climb heaven's height, and bring a blessing down.

Joanna Baillie

The Bible is the only source of all Christian truth;—the only rule for the Christian life;—the only book that unfolds to us the realities of eternity. There is no book like the Bible for excellent wisdom and use.

Sir Matthew Hale

To a certain extent, God gives to the prayerful control of Himself, and becomes their willing agent; and when the time comes when all mysteries are solved, and the record of all lives is truthfully revealed, it will probably be seen that not those who astonished the world with their own powers, but those who quietly, through prayer, used God's power, were the ones who made the world move forward.

Edward P. Roe

The incongruity of the Bible with the age of its birth, its freedom from earthly mixtures, its original, unborrowed, solitary greatness, the suddenness with which it broke forth amidst the general gloom, these, to me, are strong indications of its Divine descent: I cannot reconcile them with a human origin.

William Ellery Channing

Bad men or devils would not have written the Bible, for it condemns them and their works;—good men or angels could not have written it, for in saying it was from God when it was but their own invention, they would have been guilty of falsehood, and thus could not have been good, the only remaining being who could have written it, is God—its real author. The Scriptures teach us the best way of living, the noblest way of suffering, and the most comfortable way of dying.

John Flavel

The Gospel is not merely a book—it is a living power—a book surpassing all others.— I never omit to read it, and every day with the same pleasure. Nowhere is to be found such a series of beautiful ideas, and admirable moral maxims, which pass before us like the battalions of a celestial army. The soul can never go astray with this book for its guide.

Napoleon Bonaparte

As my greatest business is for God, to serve him, so my daily business is with God, to ask him for strength to do it.

Author Unknown

Scholars may quote Plato in their studies, but the hearts of millions will quote the Bible at their daily toil, and draw strength from its inspirations, as the meadows draw it from the brook.

Moncure Daniel Conway

The Bible is the light of my understanding, the joy of my heart, the fullness of my hope, the clarifier of my affections, the mirror of my thoughts, the consoler of my sorrows, the guide of my soul through this gloomy labyrinth of time, the telescope sent from heaven to reveal to the eye of man the amazing glories of the far distant world. The Bible contains more true sublimity, more exquisite beauty, more precise morality, more important history, and finer strains of poetry and eloquence, than can be collected from all other books, in whatever age or language they may have been written.

Sir William Jones

So great is my veneration for the Bible, that the earlier my children begin to read it the more confident will be my hopes that they will prove useful citizens to their country and respectable members of society.

John Quincy Adams

I have always said, I always will say, that the studious perusal of the sacred volume will make better citizens, better fathers, and better husbands.

Thomas Jefferson

The first petition that we are to make to Almighty God is for a good conscience, the next for health of mind, and then of body.

Lucius Annaeus Seneca

It is a belief in the Bible, the fruit of deep meditation, which has served me as the guide of my moral and literary life.—I have found it a capital safely invested and richly productive of interest.

Johann Wolfgang von Goethe

A song will outlive all sermons in the memory.

Henry Giles

In what light soever we regard the Bible, whether with reference to revelation, to history, or to morality, it is an invaluable and inexhaustible mine of knowledge and virtue.

John Quincy Adams

The general diffusion of the Bible is the most effectual way to civilize and humanize mankind, to purify and exalt the general system of public morals, to give efficacy to the just precepts of international and municipal law, to enforce the observance of prudence, temperance, justice and fortitude, and to improve all the relations of social and domestic life.

Chancellor Kent

The Bible goes equally to the cottage of the peasant, and the palace of the king.— It is woven into literature, and colors the talk of the street.—The bark of the merchant cannot sail without it; and no ship of war goes to the conflict but it is there.—It enters men's closets, directs their conduct, and mingles in all the grief and cheerfulness of life.

Theodore Parker

If one draws near to God with praise and prayer even half a cubit foot, God will go twenty leagues to meet him.

Sir Edwin Arnold

The Bible is one of the greatest blessings bestowed by God on the children of men.—It has God for its author, salvation for its end, and truth without any mixture for its matter.—It is all pure, all sincere, nothing too much, nothing wanting.

John Locke

Just as all things upon earth represent and image forth all the realities of another world, so the Bible is one mighty representative of the whole spiritual life of humanity.

Helen Keller

The Bible rose to the place it now occupies because it deserved to rise to that place, and not because God sent anybody with a box of tricks to prove its divine authority.

Bruce Barton

Voltaire spoke of the Bible as a short-lived book. He said that within a hundred years it would pass from common use. Not many people read Voltaire today, but his house has been packed with Bibles as a depot of a Bible society.

Bruce Barton

I know the Bible is inspired because it finds me at greater depths of my being than any other book.

Samuel Taylor Coleridge

There never was found, in any age of the world, either religion or law that did so highly exalt the public good as the Bible.

Francis Bacon

The nature of Christ's existence is mysterious, I admit; but his mystery meets the wants of man.—Reject it and the world is an inexplicable riddle; believe it, and the history of our race is satisfactorily explained.

Napoleon Bonaparte

I have always believed in the inspiration of the Holy Scriptures, whereby they have become the expression to man of the Word and Will of God.

Warren G. Harding

I cannot too greatly emphasize the importance and value of Bible study—more important than ever before in these days of uncertainties, when men and women are apt to decide questions from the standpoint of expediency rather than on the eternal principles laid down by God, Himself.

John Wanamaker

When you have read the Bible, you will know it is the word of God, because you will have found it the key to your own duty.

Thomas Woodrow Wilson

The most learned, acute, and diligent student cannot, in the longest life, obtain an entire knowledge of this one volume [the Bible]. The more deeply he works the mine, the richer and more abundant he finds the ore; new light continually beams from this source of heavenly knowledge, to direct the conduct, and illustrate the work of God and the ways of men; and he will at last leave the world confessing, that the more he studied the Scriptures, the fuller conviction he had of his own ignorance, and of their inestimable value.

Walter Dill Scott

My heart has always assured and reassured me that the gospel of Christ must be a Divine reality.—The sermon on the mount cannot be merely a human production.—The belief enters into the very depth of my conscience.—The whole history of man proves it.

Daniel Webster

The Bible is a window in this prison of hope, through which we look into eternity.

John S. Dwight

I speak as a man of the world to men of the world; and I say to you, search the scriptures! The Bible is the book of all others, to be read at all ages, and in all conditions of human life; not to be read once or twice or thrice through, and then laid aside, but to be read in small portions of one or two chapters every day, and never to be intermitted, unless by some overruling necessity.

John Quincy Adams

Sink the Bible to the bottom of the ocean, and still man's obligations to God would be unchanged.—He would have the same path to tread, only his lamp and his guide would be gone;—the same voyage to make, but his chart and compass would be overboard.

Henry Ward Beecher

The grand old Book of God still stands, and this old earth, the more its leaves are turned over and pondered, the more it will sustain and illustrate the sacred Word.

James Dwight Dana

That the truths of the Bible have the power of awakening an intense moral feeling in every human being; that they make bad men good, and send a pulse of healthful feeling through all the domestic, civil, and social relations; that they teach men to love right, and hate wrong, and seek each other's welfare as children of a common parent; that they control the baleful passions of the heart, and thus make men proficient in self-government; and finally, that they teach man to aspire after conformity to a being of infinite holiness, and fill him with hopes more purifying, exalted, and suited to his nature than any other book the world has ever known—these are facts as incontrovertible as the laws of philosophy, or the demonstrations of mathematics.

Francis Wayland

To say nothing of its holiness or authority, the Bible contains more specimens of genius and taste than any other volume in existence.

Walter Savage Landor

Hold fast to the Bible as the anchor of your liberties; write its precepts in your hearts, and practice them in your lives. To the influence of this book we are indebted for all the progress made in true civilization, and to this we must look as our guide in the future. "Righteousness exalteth a nation; but sin is a reproach to any people."

Ulysses S. Grant

A loving trust in the Author of the Bible is best preparation for a wise and profitable study of the Bible itself.

Henry Clay Trumbull

One monarch to obey, one creed to own, that monarch God, that creed his word alone. If there is any one fact or doctrine, or command, or promise in the Bible which has produced no practical effect on your temper, or heart, or conduct, be assured you do not truly believe it.

Edward Payson

A noble book! All men's book! It is our first, oldest statement of the never-ending problem;—man's destiny, and God's ways with him here on earth, and all in such free-flowing outlines,—grand in its sincerity, in its simplicity, and its epic melody.

Thomas Carlyle

Did you ever notice that while the gospel sets before us a higher and more blessed heaven than any other religion, its hell is also deeper and darker than any other?

Samuel Warren

It is not talking but walking that will bring us to heaven.

Matthew Henry

All that I am I owe to Jesus Christ, revealed to me in His divine Book.
David Livingstone

Do you know a book that you are willing to put under your head for a pillow when you lie dying? That is the book you want to study while you are living. There is but one such book in the world.

Joseph Cook

After all, the Bible must be its own argument and defense. The power of it can never be proved unless it is felt. The authority of it can never be supported unless it is manifest. The light of it can never be demonstrated unless it shines.

Henry Van Dyke

I have read the Bible through many times, and now make it a practice to read it through once every year.—It is a book of all others for lawyers, as well as divines; and I pity the man who cannot find in it a rich supply of thought and of rules for conduct.

Daniel Webster

Before I translated the New Testament out of the Greek, all longed after it; when it was done, their longing lasted scarce four weeks. Then they desired the books of Moses; when I had translated these, they had enough thereof in a short time. After that, they would have the Psalms; of these they were soon weary, and desired other books. So it will be with the book of Ecclesiastes, which they now long for, and about which I have taken great pains. All is acceptable until our giddy brains be satisfied; afterwards we let familiar things lie, and seek after new.

Martin Luther

The morality of the Bible is, after all, the safety of society.

Francis Cassette Monfort

The shifting systems of false religion are continually changing their places; but the gospel of Christ is the same forever. While other false lights are extinguished, this true light ever shineth.

Theodore Ledyard Cuyler

What can be more foolish than to think that all this rare fabric of heaven and earth could come by chance, when all the skill of art is not able to make an oyster.

Jeremy Taylor

Nobody ever outgrows Scripture; the book widens and deepens with our years.

Charles Haddon Spurgeon

In the long run, morals without religion, will wither and die like seed sown upon stony ground, or among thorns.

Author Unknown

So comprehensive are the doctrines of the gospel, that they involve all moral truth known by man; so extensive are the precepts, that they require every virtue, and forbid every sin. Nothing has been added, either by the labors of philosophy or the progress of human knowledge.

Author Unknown

By desiring what is perfectly good, even when we do not quite know what it is, and cannot do what we would, we are part of the divine power against evil, widening the skirts of light and making the struggle with darkness narrower.

George Eliot

Men are not made religious by performing certain actions which are externally good, but they must first have righteous principles, and then they will not fail to perform virtuous actions.

Martin Luther

The highest earthly enjoyments are but a shadow of the joy I find in reading God's word.

Lady Jane Grey

Infidelity is the joint offspring of an irreligious temper and unholy speculation, employed not in examining the evidences of Christianity, but in detecting the vices and imperfections of professing Christians.

Jeremy Taylor

They that cry down moral honesty, cry down that which is a great part of my religion, my duty toward God, and my duty toward man. What care I to see a man run after a sermon, if he cozens and cheats as soon as he comes home. On the other side, morality must not be without religion; for if so, it may change, as I see convenience. Religion must govern it. He that has not religion to govern his morality, is no better than my mastiff dog; so long as you stroke him, and please him, he will play with you as finely as may be; he is a very good moral mastiff; but if you hurt him, he will fly in your face, and tear out your throat.

John Selden

The morality which is divorced from godliness, however specious and captivating to the eye, is superficial and deceptive. The only morality that is clear in its source, pure in its precepts, and efficacious in its influence, is the morality of the gospel. All else is, at best, but idolatry—the worship of something of man's own creation; and that imperfect and feeble, like himself, and wholly insufficient to give him support and strength.

John Sergeant

All sects are different, because they come from men; morality is everywhere the same, because it comes from God.

Francois Marie de Voltaire

There is a Book worth all other books which were ever printed.

Patrick Henry

All moral obligation resolves itself into the obligation of conformity to the will of God.

Charles Hodge

Christian morality assumes to itself no merit—it sets up no arrogant claim to God's favor—it pretends not to "open the gates of heaven"; it is only the handmaid in conducting the Christian believer in his road toward them.

Richard Mant

The Word of God will stand a thousand readings; and he who has gone over it most frequently is the surest of finding new wonders there.

James Hamilton

In Christianity there can be no divorce of religion from morality.—Justification and sanctification are forever united.— The heathen notion of religion as something apart from moral life, is forever thrust out of sight by the Gospel.

Milton Valentine

There are many that say, "Give us the morality of the New Testament; never mind about the theology." Aye, but you cannot get the morality without the theology, unless you like to have rootless flowers and lamps without oil. And if you want to live as Paul enjoins, you will have to believe as Paul preaches.

Author Unknown

There is no true abiding morality that is not founded in religion.

Henry Ward Beecher

113

The morality of the gospel is the noblest gift ever bestowed by God on man.

Charles de Secondat Montesquieu

In all ranks of life the human heart yearns for the beautiful; and the beautiful things that God makes are his to give to all alike.

Harriett Beecher Stowe

When I was young I was sure of everything; in a few years, having been mistaken a thousand times, I was not so sure of most things as I was before; as present, I am hardly sure of anything but what God has revealed to me.

John Wesley

He is of the earth, but his thoughts are with the stars. Mean and petty his wants and desires; yet they serve a soul exalted with grand, glorious aims,—with immortal longings,—with thoughts which sweep the heavens, and wander through eternity. A pigmy standing on the outward crest of this small planet, his far-reaching spirit stretches outward to the infinite, and there alone finds rest.

Thomas Carlyle

You little know what you have done, when you have first broke the bounds of modesty; you have set open the door of your fancy to the devil, so that he can, almost at his pleasure ever after, represent the same sinful pleasure to you anew; he hath now access to your fancy to stir up lustful thoughts and desires, so that when you should think of your calling, of your God, or of your soul, your thoughts will be worse than swinish, upon the filth that is not fit to be named. If the devil here get in a foot, he will not easily be got out.

Richard Baxter

In contemplation of created things, by steps we may ascend to God.

John Milton

The highest morality, if not inspired and vitalized by religion, is but as the marble statue, or the silent corpse, to the living and perfect man.

Samuel I. Prime

Beauty is but the sensible image of the Infinite.—Like truth and justice it lives within us; like virtue and the moral law it is a companion of the soul.

George Bancroft

We shall never wander from Christ while we make character the end and aim of all our intellectual discipline; and we shall never misconceive character while we hold fast to Christ, and keep him first in our motto and our hearts.

Sylvester Scovel

No human face is exactly the same in its lines on each side; no leaf is perfect in its halves, and no branch in its symmetry.— All admit irregularity, as they imply change.—To banish imperfection is to destroy expression, to check exertion, to paralyze vitality.—All things are better, lovelier, and more beloved for the imperfections which have been divinely appointed, that the law of human life may be effort, and the law of human judgment may be mercy.

John Ruskin

Of all our losses, those delay doth cause, are most and heaviest.—By it oft we lose the richest treasures, knowledge, wealth, and power, and oft, alas! the never dying soul.—The calls of God and duty we intend to hear, at some convenient season, which to us may never come.—And thus we madly waste probation, forfeit heaven, and heedless sink to endless death.

Tryon Edwards

Our headstrong passions shut the door of our souls against God.
Confucius

115

He that takes his cares on himself loads himself in vain with an uneasy burden.—I will cast my cares on God; he has bidden me; they cannot burden him.

Bishop Joseph Hall

No affliction nor temptation, no guilt nor power of sin, no wounded spirit nor terrified conscience, should induce us to despair of help and comfort from God.

Thomas Scott

Speculate not too much on the mysteries of truth or providence.—The effort to explain everything, sometimes may endanger faith.—Many things God reserves to himself, and many are reserved for the unfoldings of the future life.

Tryon Edwards

No more fatal error can be cherished than that any character can be complete without the religious element. The essential factors in character building are religion, morality, and knowledge.

Josiah Little Pickard

Many flowers open to the sun, but only one follows him constantly.—Heart, be thou the sunflower, not only open to receive God's blessing, but constant in looking to him.

Jean Paul Richter

The best school of nobility is the imitation of Christ.
Frederick D. Huntington

If thou neglectest thy love to thy neighbor, in vain thou professest thy love to God; for by thy love to God, the love to thy neighbor is begotten, and by the love to thy neighbor, thy love to God is nourished.

Francis Quarles

I would fain know all that I need, and all that I may.—I leave God's secrets to himself.—It is happy for me that God makes me of his court, and not of his council.

Bishop Joseph Hall

God is everywhere, the God who framed mankind to be one mighty family, Himself our Father, and the world our home.

Hartley Coleridge

No father or mother has loved you as God has, for it was that you might be happy he gave his only son.

Henry Wadsworth Longfellow

Love is the greatest thing that God can give us, for [he] himself is love; and it is the greatest thing we can give to God, for it will also give ourselves, and carry with it all that is ours. The apostle calls it the bond of perfection; it is the old, the new, and the great commandment, and all the commandments, for it is the fulfilling of the law. It does the work of all the other graces without any instrument but its own immediate virtue.

Jeremy Taylor

The Jews ruin themselves at their passover; the Moors, at their marriages; and the Christians, in their lawsuits.

Spanish Proverb

There is no philanthropy equal to that which the gospel plants in the human heart.—It turns the severest sacrifices for Christ and humanity into pleasures, and enriches the soul with impulses and aspirations that grow only in the soil of love.

Independent

Allah obligeth no man to more than he hath given him ability to perform.

The Koran

God, veiled in majesty, alone gives light and life to all; bids the great systems move, and changing seasons in their turns advance, unmoved, unchanged himself.

Thomas Somerville

Nature and revelation are like God's books; each may have mysteries, but in each there are plain practical lessons for every-day duty.

Tryon Edwards

Failure is often God's own tool for carving some of the finest outlines in the character of his children; and, even in this life, bitter and crushing failures have often in them the germs of new and quite unimagined happiness.

Thomas Hodgkin

Heaven-born, the soul a heavenward course must hold; beyond the world she soars; the wise man, I affirm, can find no rest in that which perishes, nor will he lend his heart to aught that doth on time depend.

Michelangelo

Millions of spiritual creatures walk the earth unseen, both when we sleep and when we wake.

John Milton

I can make a lord, but only the Almighty can make a gentleman.

King James I

Heaven is large and affords space for all modes of love and fortitude.

Ralph Waldo Emerson

Walk in the light and thou shalt see thy path, though thorny, bright; for God, by grace, shall dwell in thee, and God himself is light.

Bernard Barton

118

No man will go to heaven when he dies who has not sent his heart thither while he lives. Our greatest security is to be derived from duty, and our only confidence from the mercy of God through Jesus Christ.

Daniel Wilson

The burning conviction that we have a holy duty toward others is often a way of attaching our frowning selves to a passing raft.

Eric Hoffer

One of the hardest lessons we have to learn in this life, and the one that many persons never learn, is to see the divine, the celestial, the pure in the common, the near at hand,—to see that heaven lies about us here in this world.

John Burroughs

The light of nature, the light of science, and the light of reason, are but as darkness compared with the divine light which shines only from the word of God.

John R. Lord

In the spiritual world no one is permitted to think and will in one way and speak and act in other.

Emanuel Swedenborg

Prosperity is the blessing of the Old Testament; adversity of the New, which carrieth the greater benediction and the clearer revelation of God's favor. Prosperity is not without many fears and distastes; adversity not without many comforts and hopes.

Francis Bacon

Do not ask God the way to heaven; he'll show you the hardest way.

Leszinski Stanislas

He that studies to know duty, and labors in all things to do it, will have two heavens—one of joy, peace, and comfort on earth, and the other of glory and happiness beyond the grave.

Author Unknown

The eye's light is a noble gift of heaven! All beings live from light; each fair created thing, the very plants, turn with a joyful transport to the light.

Johann Christoph Friedrich von Schiller

The generous who is always just, and the just who is always generous, may, unannounced, approach the throne of heaven.

John Caspar Lavater

A good man is influenced by God himself, and has a kind of divinity within him; so it may be a question whether he goes to heaven, or heaven comes to him.

Lucius Annaeus Seneca

The first creation of God, in the works of the days, was the light of sense; the last was the light of reason; and his Sabbath work, ever since, is the illumination of the spirit.

Francis Bacon

Man should be ever better than he seem; and shape his acts, and discipline his mind, to walk adorning earth, with hope of heaven.

Sir Aubrey de Vere

Earth hath no sorrow that heaven cannot heal.
Sir Thomas Moore

As grace is first from God, so it is continually from him, as much as light is all day long from the sun, as well as at first dawn or at sun-rising.

Jonathan Edwards

He who has no mind to trade with the devil, should be so wise as to keep away from his shop.

Robert South

So weak is man, so ignorant and blind, that did not God sometimes withhold in mercy what we ask, we should be ruined at our own request.

Hannah More

"Hell is paved with good intentions," says Johnson.—Better say the way to it is.

Author Unknown

Preventives of evil are far better than remedies; cheaper and easier of application, and surer in result.

Tryon Edwards

Many think themselves to be truly God-fearing when they call this world a valley of tears. But I believe they would be more so, if they called it a happy valley. God is more pleased with those who think everything right in the world, than with those who think nothing right. With so many thousand joys, it is not ingratitude to call the world a place of sorrow and torment?

Jean Paul Richter

Hail! Holy light, offspring of heaven, first born!
John Milton

There are two unalterable prerequisites to man's being happy in the world to come. His sins must be pardoned and his nature must be changed. He must have a title to heaven and a fitness for heaven. These two ideas underlie the whole of Christ's work, and without the title to, and the fitness for, no man can enter the kingdom of God.

John Robert Seeley

Poverty is not always of the nature of an affliction or judgment, but is rather merely a state of life, appointed by God for the proper trial and exercise of the virtues of contentment, patience, and resignation; and for one man to murmur against God, because he possesses not the riches he has given to another, is "the wrath that killeth the foolish man, and the envy that slayeth the silly one."

James Burgh

The more perfect the sight is the more delightful the beautiful object. The more perfect the appetite, the sweeter the food. The more musical the ear, the more pleasant the melody. The more perfect the soul, the more joyous the joys of heaven and the more glorious that glory.

Richard Baxter

We are what we are; we cannot be truly other than ourselves. We reach perfection not by copying, much less by aiming at originality, but by constantly and steadily working out the life which is common to all, according to the character which God has given us.

Author Unknown

Be not overcome by evil
but overcome evil with good.

Romans 12:20

Labor to keep alive in your heart that little spark of celestial fire called conscience.

George Washington

If I am faithful to the duties of the present, God will provide for the future.

Gregory T. Bedell

Intense study of the Bible will keep any man from being vulgar in point of style.

William Hart Coleridge

If God hath made this world so fair,
where sin and death abound,
how beautiful, beyond compare,
will paradise be found!

Robert Montgomery

Never think that God's delays are God's denials. Hold on; hold fast; hold out. Patience is genius.

Georges Louis Buffon

The sincere and earnest approach of the Christian throne of the Almighty teaches the best lesson of patience under affliction, since wherefore should we mock the Deity with supplications, when we insult him by murmuring under his decrees?

Walter Dill Scott

The devil loves nothing better than the intolerance of reformers, and dreads nothing so much as their charity and patience.

James Russell Lowell

God may not give us the trivial things we pray for, but that which is far better—patience, and the development of faculties, and eternity for the use of the powers well schooled on earth.

Author Unknown

He who prays as he ought, will endeavor to live as he prays.
John Owen

123

Obedience to God is the most infallible evidence of sincere and supreme love to him.

Nathaniel Emmons

There are times when God asks nothing of his children except silence, patience, and tears.

Charles Seymour Robinson

We are born subjects, and to obey God is perfect liberty. He that does this shall be free, safe, and happy.

Lucius Annaeus Seneca

Let the ground of all religious actions be obedience; examine not why it is commanded, but observe it because it is commanded. True obedience neither procrastinates nor questions.

Francis Quarles

God walks with the humble; he reveals himself to the lowly; he gives understanding to the little ones; he discloses his meaning to pure minds, but hides his grace from the curious and the proud.

Thomas á Kempis

The Stoic philosophy insults human nature, and discourages all our attempts, by enjoining and promising a perfection in this life, of which we feel ourselves incapable. The Christian religion shows compassion to our weakness, by prescribing to us only the practical task of aiming continually at further improvements and animates our endeavors, by the promise of divine aid, equal to our trial.

Author Unknown

The honest man's the noblest work of God.

Alexander Pope

He who loves goodness harbors angels, reveres reverence, and lives with God.

Ralph Waldo Emerson

There is but one road to lead us to God—humility; all other ways would only lead astray, even were they fenced in with all virtues.

Nicolas Boileau

The first law that ever God gave to man, was a law of obedience; it was a commandment pure and simple, therein man had nothing to inquire after or to dispute, for as much as to obey is the proper office of a rational soul acknowledging a heavenly superior and benefactor.—From obedience and submission spring all other virtues, as all sin does from self-opinion and self-will.

Michel E. de Montaigne

The gospel in all its doctrines and duties appears infinitely superior to any human composition.—It has no mark of human ignorance, imperfection, or sinfulness, but bears the signature of divine wisdom, authority, and importance, and is most worthy of the supreme attention and regard of all intelligent creatures.

Nathaniel Emmons

Patient waiting is often the highest way of doing God's will.
Jeremy Collier

We must never undervalue any person.—The workman loves not to have his work despised in his presence. Now God is present everywhere, and every person is his work.

Saint Francis de Sales

The books of Nature and of Revelation equally elevate our conceptions and invite our piety; they are both written by the finger of the one eternal, incomprehensible God.

Thomas Watson

Send your audience away with a desire for, and an impulse toward spiritual improvement, or your preaching will be a failure.

Edward M. Goulburn

There is not a book on earth so favorable to all the kind and to all the sublime affections, or so unfriendly to hatred, persecution, tyranny, injustice, and every sort of malevolence as the gospel.—It breathes, throughout, only mercy, benevolence, and peace.

James Beattie

Too many have no idea of the subjection of their temper to the influence of religion, and yet what is changed if the temper is not? If a man is as passionate, malicious, resentful, sullen, moody, or morose after his conversion as before it, what is he converted from or to?

John Angell James

The good are heaven's peculiar care.

Ovid

The whole hope of human progress is suspended on the ever-growing influence of the Bible.

William H. Seward

I search in vain in history to find the similar to Jesus Christ, or anything which can approach the gospel.—Neither history, nor humanity, nor the ages, nor nature offer me anything with which I am able to compare or explain it.—There is nothing there which is not beyond the march of events and above the human mind.—What happiness it gives to those who believe it! What marvels there are for those who admire and reflect upon it!

Napoleon Bonaparte

Real goodness does not attach itself merely to this life—it points to another world. Political or professional reputation cannot last forever, but in a conscience void of offense before God and man is an inheritance for eternity.

Daniel Webster

We can learn nothing of the gospel except by feeling its truths. There are some sciences that may be learned by the head, but the science of Christ crucified can only be learned by the heart.

Charles Haddon Spurgeon

There may be a certain pleasure in vice, but there is a higher in purity and virtue.—The most commanding of all delights is the delight in goodness.—The beauty of holiness is but one beauty, but it is the highest.—It is the loss of the sense of sin and shame that destroys both men and states.

Independent

There is a peculiar beauty about godly old age—the beauty of holiness.

Alexander Smith

Danger past, God is forgotten.

Thomas Fuller

It is not a minister's wisdom but his conviction which imparts itself to others. Nothing gives life but life. Real flame alone kindles other flame; this was the power of the apostles: "We believe and therefore speak." Firm faith in what they spoke, that was the basis of the apostles' strength.

Frederick William Robertson

He that loseth wealth, loseth much; he that loseth friends, loseth more; but he that loseth his spirit, loseth all.

Spanish Maxim

LITERATURE AND LIFE

Let us pity those poor rich men who live barrenly in great bookless houses! Let us congratulate the poor that, in our day, books are so cheap that a man may every year add a hundred volumes to his library for the price of what his tobacco and beer would cost him. Among the earliest ambitions to be excited in clerks, workmen, journeymen, and, indeed, among all that are struggling up from nothing to something, is that of owning, and constantly adding to a library of good books. A little library, growing larger every year, is an honorable part of a young man's history. It is a man's duty to have books. A library is not a luxury, but one of the necessaries of life.

Henry Ward Beecher

Read no history: read nothing but biography, for that is life without theory.

Benjamin Disraeli

Generally speaking an author's style is a faithful copy of his mind. If you would write a lucid style, let there first be light in your own mind; and if you would write a grand style, you ought to have a grand character.

Johann Wolfgang von Goethe

Books are the true levellers.—They give to all who faithfully use them, the society, the spiritual presence of the greatest and best of our race.

William Ellery Channing

Few are sufficiently sensible of the importance of that economy in reading which selects, almost exclusively, the very first order of books. Why, except for some special reason, read an inferior book, at the very time you might be reading one of the highest order?

John Foster

A bad book is the worse that it cannot repent.—It has not been the devil's policy to keep the masses of mankind in ignorance; but finding that they will read, he is doing all in his power to poison their books.

Edward N. Kirk

The two most engaging powers of an author, are, to make new things familiar, and familiar things new.

Samuel Johnson

When a book raises your spirit, and inspires you with noble and manly thoughts, seek for no other test of its excellence.—It is good, and made by a good workman.

Jean de la Bruyére

Bad books are like intoxicating drinks; they furnish neither nourishment, nor medicine.—Both improperly excite; the one the mind; the other the body.—The desire for each increases by being fed.—Both ruin; one the intellect; the other the health; and together, the soul.—The safeguard against each is the same— total abstinence from all that intoxicates either mind or body.

Tryon Edwards

True glory consists in doing what deserves to be written; in writing what deserves to be read; and in so living as to make the world happier and better for our living in it.

Pliny

To use books rightly, is to go to them for help; to appeal to them when our own knowledge and power fail; to be led by them into wider sight and purer conception than our own, and to receive from them the united sentence of the judges and councils of all time, against our solitary and unstable opinions.

John Ruskin

A house without books is like a room without windows. No man has a right to bring up his children without surrounding them with books, if he has the means to buy them. It is a wrong to his family. Children learn to read by being in the presence of books.

Horace Mann

The constant habit of perusing devout books is so indispensable, that it has been termed the oil of the lamp of prayer. Too much reading, however, and too little meditation, may produce the effect of a lamp inverted; which is extinguished by the very excess of that aliment, whose property is to feed it.

Hannah More

Books are but waste paper unless we spend in action the wisdom we get from thought.
Edward George Bulwer-Lytton

The love of knowledge comes with reading and grows upon it. And the love of knowledge, in a young mind, is almost a warrant against the inferior excitement of passions and vices.

Henry Ward Beecher

The books that help you most, are those which make you think the most.—The hardest way of learning is that of easy reading; but a great book that comes from a great thinker is a ship of thought, deeply freighted with truth and beauty.

Theodore Parker

The last thing that we discover in writing a book, is to know what to put at the beginning.

Blaise Pascal

The books we read should be chosen with great care, that they may be, as an Egyptian king wrote over his library, "The medicines of the soul." Be as careful of the books you read, as of the company you keep; for your habits and character will be as much influenced by the former as by the latter.

Edwin Paxton Hood

We ought to reverence books; to look on them as useful and mighty things.—If they are good and true, whether they are about religion, politics, farming, trade, law, or medicine, they are the message of Christ, the maker of all things—the teacher of all truth.

Charles Kingsley

Choose an author as you choose a friend.

Wentworth D. Roscommon

If all the crowns of Europe were placed at my disposal on condition that I should abandon my books and studies, I should spurn the crowns away and stand by the books.

Bishop Francis de S. Fenelon

The silent influence of books is a mighty power in the world; and there is a joy in reading them known only to those who read them with desire and enthusiasm.—Silent, passive, and noiseless though they be, they yet set in action countless multitudes, and change the order of nations.

Henry Giles

Books, like friends, should be few and well chosen. Like friends, too, we should return to them again and again—for, like true friends, they will never fail us—never cease to instruct— never cloy.—Next to acquiring good friends, the best acquisition is that of good books.

Caleb C. Colton

Many books require no thought from those who read them, and for a very simple reason; they made no such demand upon those who wrote them. Those works, therefore, are the most valuable, that set our thinking faculties in the fullest operation.

Caleb C. Colton

The student has his Rome, his Florence, his whole glowing Italy, within the four walls of his library. He has in his books the ruins of an antique world and the glories of a modern one.

Henry Wadsworth Longfellow

Every good writer has much idiom; it is the life and spirit of language.

Walter Savage Landor

No possession can surpass, or even equal a good library, to the lover of books. Here are treasured up for his daily use and delectation, riches which increase by being consumed, and pleasures which never cloy.

John Alfred Langford

When I get a little money, I buy books; and if any is left, I buy food and clothes.
Desiderius Erasmus

135

Consider what you have in the smallest chosen library. A company of the wisest and wittiest men that could be picked out of all civil countries, in a thousand years, have set in best order the results of their learning and wisdom. The men themselves were hid and inaccessible, solitary, impatient of interruption, fenced by etiquette; but the thought which they did not uncover to their bosom friend is here written out in transparent words to us, the strangers of another age.

Ralph Waldo Emerson

What a world of wit is here packed together!—I know not whether the sight doth more dismay or comfort me.—it dismays me to think that here is so much I cannot know; it comforts me to think that this variety yields so good helps to know what I should.—Blessed be the memory of those who have left their blood, their spirits, their lives, in these precious books, and have willingly wasted themselves into these during monuments, to give light unto others.

Bishop Joseph Hall

The literature of a people must spring from the sense of its nationality; and nationality is impossible without self-respect, and self-respect is impossible without liberty.

Harriet Beecher Stowe

The great standard of literature, as to purity and exactness of style, is the Bible.

Hugh Blair

There is no worse robber than a bad book.
Italian Proverb

Language is a solemn thing: it grows out of life—out of its agonies and ecstasies, its wants and its weariness.—Every language is a temple in which the soul of those who speak it is enshrined.

Oliver Wendell Holmes

From this slender beginning I have gradually formed a numerous and select library, the foundation of all my works, and the best comfort of my life, both at home and abroad.

Edward Gibbon

A library may be regarded as the solemn chamber in which a man may take counsel with all who have been wise, and great, and good, and glorious among the men that have gone before him.

George Dawson

We enter our studies, and enjoy a society which we alone can bring together. We raise no jealousy by conversing with one in preference to another: we give no offense to the most illustrious by questioning him as long as we will, and leaving him as abruptly. Diversity of opinion raises no tumult in our presence; each interlocutor stands before us, speaks or is silent, and we adjourn or decide the business at our leisure.

Walter Savage Landor

No habitual reader of the common run of novels can love the Bible or any other book that demands thought, or inculcates the serious duties of life. He dwells in a region of imagination, where he is disgusted with the plainness and simplicity of truth, and with the sober realities that demand his attention as a rational and immortal being, and an accountable subject of God's government.

Author Unknown

In the literature of the world there is not one popular book which is immoral that continues to exist two centuries after it is produced; for in the heart of nations the false does not live so long, and the true is ethical to the end of time.

Edward George Bulwer-Lytton

The true university of these days is a collection of books.

Thomas Carlyle

A beautiful literature springs from the depth and fullness of intellectual and moral life, from an energy of thought and feeling, to which nothing, as we believe, ministers so largely as enlighted religion.

William Ellery Channing

Language was given us that we might say pleasant things to each other.

Christian Nestell Bovee

We must have books for recreation and entertainment, as well as for instruction and for business; the former are agreeable, the latter useful, and the human mind requires both. The canon law and the codes of Justinian shall have due honor and reign at the universities, but Homer and Virgil need not therefore be banished. We will cultivate the olive and the vine, but without eradicating the myrtle and the rose.

Honoré de Balzac

Books only partially represent their authors; the writer is always greater than his work.

Christian Nestell Bovee

The decline of literature indicates the decline of a nation; the two keep pace in their downward tendency.

Johann Wolfgang von Goethe

Literature happens to be the only occupation in which wages are not given in proportion to the goodness of the work done.

James A. Froude

Literature has now become a game in which the booksellers are the kings; the critics, the knaves; the public, the pack; and the poor author, the mere table or thing played upon.

Caleb C. Colton

Fiction is a potent agent for good in the hands of the good; and so it may be a potent agent for evil, according to its character and the character of its readers.

Author Unknown

Upon books the collective education of the race depends; they are the sole instruments of registering, perpetuating, and transmitting thought.

Henry Rogers

To be what we are, and to become what we are capable of becoming, is the only end of life.

Robert Louis Stevenson

Novels are mean imitations of literature, and usually the poorest part of it. They devour much precious time, and, what is worse, have a bad effect upon mind and morals. Their fanciful, distorted, and exaggerated sketches of life tend to vitiate and corrupt the taste, and to excite expectations that can never be fulfilled.

Charles Varle

A printed speech is like a dried flower: the substance, indeed, is there, but the color is faded and the perfume gone.

Paul Lorain

If I might control the literature of the household, I would guarantee the well-being of the church and state.

Francis Bacon

Three-fourths of the popular novels of the day enfeeble the intellect, impoverish the imagination, vulgarize the taste and style, give false or distorted views of life and human nature, and, which is worst of all, waste that precious time which should be given to solid mental improvement.

Greyson Letters

In literature, today, there are plenty of good masons but few good architects.

Joseph Joubert

No earnest thinker is a plagiarist pure and simple. He will never borrow from others that which he has not already, more or less, thought out for himself.

Charles Kingsley

Poetry reveals to us the loveliness of nature, brings back the freshness of youthful feeling, revives the relish of simple pleasures, keeps unquenched the enthusiasm which warmed the springtime of our being, refines youthful love, strengthens our interest in human nature, by vivid delineations of its tenderest and softest feelings, and, through the brightness of its prophetic visions, helps faith to lay hold on the future life.

William Ellery Channing

We cannot live better than in seeking to become better, nor more agreeably than in having a clear conscience.

Socrates

It is easy to criticize an author, but difficult to appreciate him.

Luc de Clapiers Vauvenargues

There are only two powers in the world, the sword and the pen; and in the end the former is always conquered by the latter.

Napoleon Bonaparte

They who have read about everything are thought to understand everything, too, but it is not always so; reading furnishes the mind only with materials of knowledge; it is thinking that makes what we read ours. We are of the ruminating kind, and it is not enough to cram ourselves with a great load of collections—we must chew them over again.

William Ellery Channing

I may hear a tale with delight, and perhaps a smile at an innocent jest, but I will not jest, nor joy at a tale disgracing an innocent person.

Arthur Warwick

A good writer is not necessarily a good book critic. No more so than a good drunk is automatically a good bartender.

Jim Bishop

If you know many people it is impossible to conduct a newspaper impersonally, and the only way to run a newspaper is in an impersonal way.

Lord Northcliffe

All journalists are, by virtue of their handicraft, alarmists; this is their way of making themselves interesting.

Lord George A. Riddell

The Jews are among the aristocracy of every land. If a literature is called rich in the possession of a few classic tragedies, what shall we say to a national tragedy, lasting for fifteen hundred years, in which the poets and actors were also the heroes?

George Eliot

The habitual indulgence in such reading, is a silent, ruining mischief.

Hannah More

A newspaper should be the maximum of information, and the minimum of comment.

Richard Cobden

A journalist is a grumbler, a censurer, a giver of advice, a regent of sovereigns, a tutor of nations. For hostile newspapers are more to be feared than a thousand bayonets.

Napoleon Bonaparte

Only actions give to life its strength, as only moderation gives it its charm.

Jean Paul Richter

Newspapers should be news-carriers, not news-makers.— There is the truth and entertainment enough to print, without fiction or falsehood, and to publish the latter is to betray the former.

Charles Simmons

Novels may teach us as wholesome a moral as the pulpit. There are "sermons in stones," in healthy books, and "good in everything."

Caleb C. Colton

BUSINESS, JOBS, AND WORK

Labor is one of the great elements of society—the great substantial interest on which we all stand. Not feudal service, or predial toil, or the irksome drudgery by one race of mankind subjected, on account of their color, to another; but labor, intelligent, manly, independent, thinking and acting for itself, earning its own wages, accumulating those wages into capital, educating childhood, maintaining worship, claiming the right of the elective franchise, and helping to uphold the great fabric of the State— that is American labor; and all my sympathies are with it, and my voice, till I am dumb, will be for it.

Daniel Webster

While the law [of competition] may be sometimes hard for the individual, it is best for the race, because it ensures the survival of the fittest in every department.

Andrew Carnegie

Corporations cannot commit treason, nor be outlawed nor excommunicated, for they have no souls.

Sir Edward Coke

We gain nothing by being with such as ourselves; we encourage each other in mediocrity.—I am always longing to be with men more excellent than myself.

Charles Lamb

The passion to get ahead is sometimes born of the fear lest we be left behind.

Eric Hoffer

If you don't crack the shell, you can't eat the nut.

Persian Proverb

Disagreeing in little things and agreeing in great ones is what forms and keeps up a commerce of society and friendship among reasonable men, and among unreasonable men breaks it.

Robert Southey

Get your facts first, and then you can distort 'em as you please.

Mark Twain

We demand that big business give people a square deal; in return we must insist that when anyone engaged in big business honestly endeavours to do right, he shall himself be given a square deal.

Theodore Roosevelt

Leisure and solitude are the best effect of riches, because [they are] the mother of thought. Both are avoided by most rich men, who seek company and business, which are signs of being weary of themselves.

Sir William Temple

In my opinion newspaper work offers better opportunities, aside from the accumulation of money, for real serviceable, result-getting labor than any other business a young man may choose.

Samuel G. Blythe

The fruit derived from labor is the sweetest of all pleasures.

Luc de Clapiers Vauvenargues

It is only by labor that thought can be made healthy, and only by thought that labor can be made happy; and the two cannot be separated with impunity.

John Ruskin

If you have built castles in the air, your work need not be lost; there is where they should be. Now put foundations under them.

Henry David Thoreau

The love of retirement has in all ages adhered closely to those minds which have been most enlarged by knowledge, or elevated by genius. Those who enjoyed everything generally supposed to confer happiness have been forced to seek it in the shades of privacy.

Samuel Johnson

There may be luck in getting a good job—but there's no luck in keeping it.

J. Ogden Armour

If you divorce capital from labor, capital is hoarded, and labor starves.

Daniel Webster

From labor, health; from health, contentment springs.

James Beattie

What men want is not talent, it is purpose; in other words, not the power to achieve, but will to labor. I believe that labor judiciously and continuously applied becomes genius.

Edward George Bulwer-Lytton

You and I toiling for earth, may at the same time be toiling for heaven, and every day's work may be a Jacob's ladder reaching up nearer to God.

Theodore Parker

Blessed is the man that has found his work.—One monster there is in the world, the idle man.

Thomas Carlyle

As steady application to work is the healthiest training for every individual, so is it the best discipline of a state. Honorable industry always travels the same road with enjoyment and duty, and progress is altogether impossible without it.

Samuel Smiles

There is a perennial nobleness and even sacredness in work.—Were he ever so benighted and forgetful of his high calling, there is always hope in a man who actually and earnestly works.

Thomas Carlyle

No abilities, however splendid, can command success without intense labor and persevering application.

Alexander T. Stewart

Labor rids us of three great evils—irksomeness, vice, and poverty.

Francois Marie de Voltaire

Nature is just toward men. It recompenses them for their sufferings; it renders them laborious, because to the greatest toils it attaches the greatest rewards.

Charles de Secondat Montesquieu

Alexander the Great, reflecting on his friends degenerating into sloth and luxury, told them that it was a most slavish thing to luxuriate, and a most royal thing to labor.

Isaac Barrow

The labor of the body relieves us from the fatigues of the mind; and this it is which forms the happiness of the poor.

Francois Duc de La Rochefoucauld

Whatever there is of greatness in the United States, or indeed in any other country, is due to labor. The laborer is the author of all greatness and wealth. Without labor there would be no government, and no leading class, and nothing to preserve.

Ulysses S. Grant

There is but one method of success, and that is hard labor.

Sydney Smith

There are many ways of being frivolous, only one way of being intellectually great; that is honest labor.

Sydney Smith

Men seldom die of hard work; activity is God's medicine. The highest genius is willingness and ability to do hard work. Any other conception of genius makes it a doubtful, if not a dangerous possession.

Robert S. MacArthur

Nothing will ever be attempted, if all possible objections must be first overcome.
Samuel Johnson

Avoid idleness, and fill up all the spaces of thy time with severe and useful employment; for lust easily creeps in at those emptinesses where the soul is unemployed and the body is at ease; for no easy, healthful, idle person was ever chaste if he could be tempted; but of all employments, bodily labor is the most useful, and of the greatest benefit for driving away the Devil.

Jeremy Taylor

Excellence in any department can be attained only by the labor of a lifetime; it is not to be purchased at a lesser price.

Samuel Johnson

The great happiness of life, I find, after all, to consist in the regular discharge of some mechanical duty.

Johann Christoph Friedrich von Schiller

Occupation was one of the pleasures of paradise, and we cannot be happy without it.

Anna Jameson

Men give me some credit for genius. All the genius I have lies just in this: When I have a subject in hand, I study it profoundly. Day and night it is before me. I explore it in all its bearings. My mind becomes pervaded with it. Then the effort which I make the people are pleased to call the fruit of genius. It is the fruit of labor and thought.

Alexander Hamilton

Labor is the great producer of wealth; it moves all other causes.

Daniel Webster

Let parents who hate their offspring rear them to hate labor and to inherit riches, and before long they will be stung by every vice, racked by its poison, and damned by its penalty.

Henry Ward Beecher

I have lived to know that the great secret of human happiness is this: never suffer your energies to stagnate. The old adage of "too many irons in the fire," conveys an abominable lie. You cannot have too many—poker, tongs, and all—keep them all going.

Adam Clarke

Too much idleness, I have observed, fills up a man's time much more completely, and leaves him less his own master, than any sort of employment whatsoever.

Edmund Burke

It is an undoubted truth, that the less one has to do the less time one finds to do it in. One yawns, one procrastinates, one can do it when one will, and, therefore, one seldom does it all; whereas those who have a great deal of business, must (to use a vulgar expression) buckle to it; and then they always find time enough to do it in.

Philip Dormer Stanhope Chesterfield

Hard workers are usually honest; industry lifts them above temptation.

Christian Nestell Bovee

Genius begins great works; labor alone finishes them.

Joseph Joubert

Five things are requisite to a good officer—ability, clean hands, despatch, patience, and impartiality.

William Penn

It is to labor and to labor only, that man owes everything of exchangeable value. Labor is the talisman that has raised him from the condition of the savage; that has changed the desert and the forest into cultivated fields; that has covered the earth with cities, and the ocean with ships; that has given us plenty, comfort, and elegance, instead of want misery, and barbarism.

John MacCulloch

We protract the career of time by employment, we lengthen the duration of our lives by wise thoughts and useful actions. Life to him who wishes not to have lived in vain is thought and action.

Johann Georg Zimmerman

You see men of the most delicate frames engaged in active and professional pursuits who really have no time for idleness. Let them become idle,—let them take care of themselves, let them think of their health,—and they die! The rust rots the steel which use preserves.

Edward George Bulwer-Lytton

Care is a sad disease; despondency a sadder, a discontent the saddest of the three: if we wish to be cured of all these together, next to seeking the divine support, the prescription is occupation.

Author Unknown

Work is a great blessing; after evil came into the world, it was given as an antidote, not as a punishment.

Arthur S. Hardy

The prosperity of a people is proportionate to the number of hands and minds usefully employed. To the community, sedition is a fever, corruption is a gangrene, and idleness is an atrophy. Whatever body or society wastes more than it acquires, must gradually decay; and every being that continues to be fed, and ceases to labor, takes away something from the public stock.

Samuel Johnson

An idle brain is the devil's workshop.

English Proverb

If ever this free people, if this government itself is ever utterly demoralized, it will come from this incessant human wriggle and struggle for office, which is but a way to live without work.

Abraham Lincoln

Laziness grows on people; it begins in cobwebs and ends in iron chains. The more business a man has to do the more he is able to accomplish, for he learns to economize his time.

Sir Matthew Hale

To be idle and to be poor have always been reproaches; and therefore every man endeavors with his utmost care to hide his poverty from others, and his idleness from himself.

Samuel Johnson

Satan selects his disciples when they are idle; but Christ chose his when they were busy at their work, either mending their nets, or casting them into the sea.

Anthony Farindon

Let a man choose what condition he will, and let him accumulate around him all the goods and gratifications seemingly calculated to make him happy in it; if that man is left at any time without occupation or amusement, and reflects on what he is, the meager, languid felicity of his present lot will not bear him up. He will turn necessarily to gloomy anticipations of the future; and unless his occupation calls him out of himself, he is inevitably wretched.

Blaise Pascal

It was a maxim with the Jews, "that he that did not bring up his son to some honest calling, brought him up to be a thief."

Author Unknown

153

Employment, which Galen calls "Nature's physician," is so essential to human happiness that indolence is justly considered as the mother of misery.

Richard E. Burton

Go to the ant, thou sluggard, learn to live, and by her busy ways, reform thine own.

Christopher Smart

Sloth makes all things difficult, but industry all easy; and he that riseth late must trot all day, and shall scarce overtake his business at night; while laziness travels so slowly that poverty soon overtakes him.

Benjamin Franklin

The way to be nothing is to do nothing.

Nathaniel Howe

Some temptations come to the industrious, but all temptations attack the idle.

Charles Haddon Spurgeon

Occupation is a necessity to the young. They love to be busy about something, however trifling; and if not directed to some useful employment will soon engage in something that is evil, thus verifying the old proverb, "That idleness is the mother of mischief."

Author Unknown

No thoroughly occupied man was ever yet very miserable.

Letitia Elizabeth Landon

There is no genius in life like the genius of energy and industry.

Donald Grant Mitchell

It would be thought a hard government that should tax its people one-tenth part of their time, to be employed in its service; but idleness taxes many of us much more; sloth, by bringing on diseases, absolutely shortens life. Sloth, like rust, consumes faster than labor wears, while the used key is always bright. Dost thou love life, then do not squander time, for that is the stuff life is made of. How much more than is necessary do we spend in sleep, forgetting that the sleeping fox catches no poultry, and there will be sleeping enough in the grave!

Benjamin Franklin

To cultivate kindness is a valuable part of the business of life.

Samuel Johnson

The career of a great man remains an enduring monument of human energy.—The man dies and disappears, but his thoughts and acts survive and leave an indelible stamp upon his race.

Samuel Smiles

Perfection consists not in doing extraordinary things, but in doing ordinary things extraordinarily well. Neglect nothing; the most trivial action may be performed to God.

Angelique Arnauld

Life is a short day; but it is a working day. Activity may lead to evil, but inactivity cannot lead to good.

Hannah More

The question "Who ought to be boss?" is like asking "Who ought to be the tenor in the quartet?" Obviously, the man who can sing tenor.

Henry Ford

Stagnation is something worse than death; it is corruption also.

William Gilmore Simms

The every-day cares and duties, which men call drudgery, are the weights and counterpoises of the clock of time, giving its pendulum a true vibration, and its hands a regular motion; and when they cease to hang upon the wheels, the pendulum no longer swings, the hands no longer move, and the clock stands still.

Henry Wadsworth Longfellow

The miracle, or the power, that elevates the few is to be found in their industry, application, and perseverance under the promptings of a brave, determined spirit.

Mark Twain

The crowning fortune of a man is to be born with a bias to some pursuit which finds him in employment and happiness.

Ralph Waldo Emerson

CHANCES, OPPORTUNITIES, AND SERENDIPITY

By going a few minutes sooner or later, by stopping to speak with a friend on the corner, by meeting this man or that, or by running down this street instead of the other, we may let slip some impending evil, by which the whole current of our lives would have been changed. There is no possible solution in the dark enigma but the one word, "Providence."

Henry Wadsworth Longfellow

There is neither vice nor virtue, there are only circumstances.

Honoré de Balzac

People are always blaming their circumstances for what they are. I don't believe in circumstances. The people who get on in this world are the people who get up and look for the circumstances they want, and, if they can't find them, make them.

George Bernard Shaw

We learn geology the morning after the earthquake.

Ralph Waldo Emerson

The wise man in the storm prays to God, not for safety from danger, but for deliverance for the fear.

Ralph Waldo Emerson

To be thrown upon one's own resources, is to be cast into the very lap of fortune; for our faculties then undergo a development and display an energy of which they were previously unsusceptible.

Benjamin Franklin

There is no such thing as chance; and what seems to us the merest accident springs from the deepest source of destiny.

Johann Christoph Friedrich von Schiller

Man is not the creature of circumstances. Circumstances are the creatures of man.

Benjamin Disraeli

Either all is chance, and being but chance is of no consequence, or God rules the world, and all is well.— Whatever befalls is just and right, and therefore not unendurable.

Andrew Lang

I never knew an early-rising, hard-working, prudent man, careful of his earnings, and strictly honest, who complained of bad luck. A good character, good habits, and iron industry are impregnable to the assaults of all the ill-luck that fools ever dreamed of.

Joseph Addison

Bad thoughts are worse enemies than lions and tigers; for we can keep out of the way of wild beasts, but bad thoughts win their way everywhere. The cup that is full will hold no more; keep your hearts full of good thoughts, that bad thoughts may find no room to enter.

Author Unknown

Fortune is ever seen accompanying industry.

Oliver Goldsmith

To be always intending to live a new life, but never to find time to set about it; this is as if a man should put off eating and drinking and sleeping from one day and night to another, till he is starved and destroyed.

John Tillotson

There is no such thing as luck. It's a fancy name for being always at our duty, and so sure to be ready when the good time comes.

Author Unknown

The least and most imperceptible impressions received in our infancy have consequences very important and of long duration.— It is with these first impressions as with a river, whose waters we can easily turn at its source; with the same facility we may turn the minds of children to what direction we please.

John Locke

Our first impressions, whether of persons or things, have great influence on all our future estimates and opinion.

Author Unknown

It takes more strength of character to withstand good fortune than bad.

Francois Duc de La Rochefoucauld

You believe easily that which you hope for earnestly.

Terence

In counsel it is good to see dangers; but in execution, not to see them unless they be very great.

Francis Bacon

I once asked a hermit in Italy how he could venture to live alone, in a single cottage, on the top of a mountain, a mile from any habitation? He replied, that Providence was his next-door neighbor.

Lawrence Sterne

In order to improve the mind, we ought less to learn, than to contemplate.

René Descartes

The great thing in the world is not so much where we stand as in what direction we are moving.

Oliver Wendell Holmes

Help thy brother's boat to yonder shore, and lo, your boat arrives also.

Chinese Proverb

What we do upon some great occasion will probably depend on what we already are: and what we are will be the result of previous years of self-discipline.

Henry P. Liddon

The conditions of conquest are always easy. We have but to toil awhile, endure awhile, believe always, and never turn back.

William Gilmore Simms

Every noble acquisition is attended with its risks; he who fears to encounter the one must not expect to obtain the other.

Pietro Metastasio

It is a law of our humanity, that man must know good through evil.—No great principle ever triumphed but through much evil.—No man ever progressed to greatness and goodness but through great mistakes.

Frederick William Robertson

Alone, man weak, tottering, yet with God this handful of dust
made to be unmade, moulded to be moldable,
grasps the ungraspable, utters the ineffable,
and when what seems too profound for
human intelligence sweeps into the
horizon, solitude is no more and misery
has departed.

Emil G. Hirsch

I bargained with life for a penny, a penny is what I got.

Anonymous

A wise man turns chance into good fortune.

Thomas Fuller

It would do the world good if every man in it would compel himself occasionally to be absolutely alone. Most of the world's progress has come out of such loneliness.

Bruce Barton

Whatever that be which thinks, which understands, which wills, which acts, it is something celestial and divine, and on that account must necessarily be eternal.

Marcus Tullius Cicero

Alas, we make a ladder of our thoughts, where angels step, but sleep ourselves at the foot; our high resolves look down upon our slumbering acts.

Letitia Elizabeth Landon

Opportunity is rare and a wise man will never let it go by him.

Bayard Taylor

There are many times and circumstances in life when "Our strength is, to sit still."

Tryon Edwards

In the end, thought rules the world. There are times when impulses and passions are more powerful, but they soon expend themselves; while mind, acting constantly, is ever ready to drive them back and work when their energy is exhausted.

James McCosh

Our grand business is not to see what lies dimly at a distance, but to do what lies clearly at hand.

Thomas Carlyle

Man must be prepared for every event of life, for there is nothing that is durable.

Menander

W hen written in Chinese the word "crisis" is composed of two characters— one represents danger and the other represents opportunity.

John F. Kennedy

Employ thy time well if thou meanest to gain leisure; and since thou art not sure of a minute, throw not away an hour. Leisure is time for doing something useful, and this leisure the diligent man will obtain, but the lazy man never, for a life of leisure and a life of laziness are two things.

Benjamin Franklin

In human life there is constant change of fortune; and it is unreasonable to expect an exemption from the common fate.— Life itself decays, and all things are daily changing.

Plutarch

The blessings of health and fortune, as they have a beginning, so they must also have an end.— Everything rises but to fall, and increases but to decay.

Sallust

How full or how empty our lives, depends, we say, on Providence. Suppose we say, more or less on improvidence.

Christan Nestell Bovee

Our greatest glory consists not in never falling, but inrising every time we fall.

Oliver Goldsmith

All nature is but art, unknown to thee; all chance, direction which thou canst not see; all discord, harmony not understood; all partial evil, universal good.

Alexander Pope

Duty and today are ours, results and futurity belong to God.

Horace Greeley

There is no one, says another, whom fortune does not visit once in his life; but when she does not find him ready to receive her, she walks in at the door, and flies out at the window.

Charles de Secondat Montesquieu

We can do more good by being good, than in any other way.

Rowland Hill

CONDUCT
AND
KINDNESS

Justice is the great interest of man on earth. It is the ligament which holds civilized beings and civilized nations together. Wherever her temple stands, and so long as it is duly honored, there is a foundation for social security, general happiness, and the improvement and progress of our race. And whoever labors on this edifice with usefulness and distinction, whoever clears its foundations, strengthens its pillars, adorns its entablatures, or contributes to raise it's august dome still higher in the skies, connects himself, in name, and fame, and character, with that which is and must be as durable as the frame of human society.

Daniel Webster

It is not enough that you form, and even follow the most excellent rules for conducting yourself in the world; you must also know when to deviate from them, and there lies the exception.

Lord Greville

I will govern my life and my thoughts as if the whole world were to see the one and read the other.—For what does it signify to make anything a secret to my neighbor, when to God, who is the searcher of our hearts, all our privacies are open.

Lucius Annaeus Seneca

The critical faculty has its value in correcting errors, reforming abuses, and demolishing superstitions.—But the constructive faculty is much nobler in itself, and immeasurably more valuable in its results, for the obvious reason that it is a much nobler and better thing to build up than to pull down.—it requires skill and labor to erect a building, but any idle tramp can burn it down.—Only God can form and paint a flower, but any foolish child can pull it to pieces.

John Monroe Gibson

It has always been more difficult for a man to keep than to get, for in one case fortune aids, as it often assists injustice; but in the other, sense is required.—Therefore we often see a person deficient in cleverness, rise in wealth; and then, from want of sense, roll head-over-heels to the bottom.

Saint Basil

Conduct is the great profession. Behavior is the perpetual revealing of us. What a man does, tells us what he is.

Frederick D. Huntington

A spirit of criticism, if indulged in, leads to a censoriousness of disposition that is destructive of all nobler feeling. The man who lives to find faults has a miserable mission.

Author Unknown

Principles last forever; but special rules pass away with the things and conditions to which they refer.

John Robert Seeley

There is scarcely a good critic of books born in our age, and yet every fool thinks himself justified in criticizing persons.

Edward George Bulwer-Lytton

We frequently fall into error and folly, not because the true principles of action are not known, but because for a time they are not remembered; he may, therefore, justly be numbered among the benefactors of mankind who contracts the great rules of life into short sentences that may early be impressed on the memory, and taught by frequent recollection to occur habitually to the mind.

Samuel Johnson

Critics are a kind of freebooters in the republic of letters, who, like deer, goats, and diverse other graminivorous animals, gain subsistence by gorging upon buds and leaves of the young shrubs of the forest, thereby robbing them of their verdure and retarding their progress to maturity.

Washington Irving

Critics must excuse me if I compare them to certain animals called asses, who, by gnawing vines, originally taught the great advantage of pruning them.

William Shenstone

The practices of good men are more subject to error than their speculations. I will, then, honor good examples, but endeavor to live according to good precepts.

Bishop Joseph Hall

The integrity of men is to be measured by their conduct, not by their professions.

Junius

171

Temper, if ungoverned, governs the whole man.

Anthony Ashley Cooper Shaftesbury

There is in some men a dispassionate neutrality of mind, which, though it generally passes for good temper, can neither gratify nor warm us; it must indeed be granted that these men can only negatively offend; but then it should also be remembered that they cannot positively please.

Lord Greville

Great objects form great minds.

Nathaniel Emmons

Man can never come up to his ideal standard.—It is the nature of the immortal spirit to raise that standard higher and higher as it goes from strength to strength, still upward and onward.—The wisest and greatest men are ever the most modest.

Sarah Margaret Fuller Ossoli

Man is unjust, but God is just; and finally justice triumphs.

Henry Wadsworth Longfellow

Justice delayed, is justice denied.

William E. Gladstone

The severest critics are always those who have either never attempted, or who have failed in original composition.

William Hazlitt

Of all mortals a critic is the silliest; for inuring himself to examine all things, whether they are of consequence or not, he never looks upon anything but with a design of passing sentence upon it; by which means he is never a companion, but always a censor.

Sir Richard Steele

Judges ought to be more learned than witty, more reverent than plausible, and more advised than confident. Above all things, integrity is their portion and proper virtue.

Francis Bacon

One man's word is no man's word; we should quietly hear both sides.

Johann Wolfgang von Goethe

We ought always to deal justly, not only with those who are just to us, but likewise to those who endeavor to injure us; and this for fear lest by rendering them evil for evil, we should fall into the same vice.

Hierocles

How can a people be free that has not learned to be just?

Abbé Sieyés

God's mill grinds slow but sure.

George Herbert

When we live habitually with the wicked, we become necessarily their victims or their disciples; on the contrary, when we associate with the virtuous we form ourselves in imitation of their virtues, or at least lose, every day, something of our faults.

Agapet

Bad temper is its own scourge. Few things are more bitter than to feel bitter. A man's venom poisons himself more than his victim.

Charles Buxton

No doubt solitude is wholesome, but so is abstinence after a surfeit. The true life of man is in society.

William Gilmore Simms

Speak the truth by all means; be bold and fearless in your rebuke of error, and in your keener rebuke of wrong doing; but be human, and loving, and gentle, and brotherly the while.

William Morley Punshon

Success, recognition, and conformity are the bywords of the modern world where everyone seems to crave the anesthetizing security of being identified with the majority.

Martin Luther King Jr.

Proportion thy charity to the strength of thine estate, lest God in anger proportion thine estate to the weakness of thy charity.

Francis Quarles

Language most shows a man; speak that I may see thee; it springs out of the most retired and inmost part of us.

Ben Jonson

Infidelity reproves nothing that is bad. It only ridicules and denounces all that is good. It tears down, but never builds up; destroys, but never imparts life; attacks religion, but offers no adequate substitute.

Joseph R. Paxton

One always receiving, never giving is like the stagnant pool, in which whatever flows remains, whatever remains corrupts.

John Angell James

Of all bad things by which mankind are curst, their own bad tempers surely are the worst.

Richard Cumberland

If a man speaks or acts with pure thought, happiness follows him like a shadow that never leaves him.

Gautama Buddha

We do not quite forgive a giver. The hand that feeds us is in some danger of being bitten.

Ralph Waldo Emerson

It is one of the most beautiful compensations of this life, that no man can sincerely try to help another without helping himself.

Author Unknown

When a person is down in the world, an ounce of help is better than a pound of preaching.

Edward George Bulwer-Lytton

Saying is one thing, doing another. We must consider the sermon and the preacher distinctly and apart.

Michel E. de Montaigne

The actions of men are like the index of a book; they point out what is most remarkable in them.

Author Unknown

Every noble activity makes room for itself.

Ralph Waldo Emerson

A life spent worthily should be measured by deeds, not years.

Richard Brinsley Sheridan

Let us not say, "Every man is the architect of his own fortune;" but let us say, "Every man is the architect of his own character."

George Dana Boardman

Our deeds determine us, as much as we determine our deeds.

George Eliot

Give us a character on which we can thoroughly depend, which we know to be based on principle and on the fear of God, and it is wonderful how many brilliant and popular and splendid qualities we can safely and gladly dispense with.

Arthur P. Stanley

If a man be endued with a generous mind, this is the best kind of nobility.

Plato

Men are not to be judged by their looks, habit, and appearances; but by the character of their lives and conversations, and by their works. 'Tis better that a man's own works than that another man's words should praise him.

Sir Roger L'Estrange

Our cares are the mothers not only of our charities and virtues, but of our best joys, and most cheering and enduring pleasures.

William Gilmore Simms

Character is perfectly educated will.

Novalis

People have a custom of excusing the enormities of their conduct by talking of their passions, as if they were under the control of a blind necessity, and sinned because they could not help it.

Richard Cumberland

Nobility, without virtue, is a fine setting without a gem.

Jane Porter

When a stupid man is doing something he is ashamed of, he always declares that it's his duty.

George Bernard Shaw

Our principles are the springs of our actions; our actions, the springs of our happiness or misery. Too much care, therefore, cannot be taken in forming our principles.

Philip Skelton

True nobility is derived from virtue, not from birth.—Title may be purchased, but virtue is the only coin that makes the bargain valid.

Richard E. Burton

Conscience! Conscience! Man's most faithful friend!

George Crabbe

Keep your conduct abreast of your conscience, and very soon your conscience will be illumined by the radiance of God.

William M. Taylor

Oh! It is excellent to have a giant's strength; but it is tyrannous to use it like a giant.

William Shakespeare

The shortest and surest way to live with honor in the world, is to be in reality what we would appear to be; and if we observe, we shall find, that all human virtues increase and strengthen themselves by the practice and experience of them.

Socrates

Do all the good you can, in all the ways you can, to all the souls you can, in every place you can, at all the times you can, with all the zeal you can, every time you can.

John Wesley

It seems to me 'tis only noble to be good.

Lord Alfred Tennyson

Great men undertake great things because they are great; fools, because they think them easy.

Luc de Clapiers Vauvenargues

He gives not best who gives most; but he gives most who gives best.—If I cannot give bountifully, yet I will give freely, and what I want in my hand, I will supply by my heart.

Arthur Warwick

Charity should be the habit of our estimates: kindness of our feelings; benevolence of our affections; cheerfulness of our social intercourse; generosity of our living; improvement of our progress; prayer of our desires; fidelity of our self-examination; being and doing good of our entire life.

Author Unknown

Never did any soul do good, but I came readier to do the same again, with more enjoyment. Never was love, or gratitude, or bounty practiced but with increasing joy, which made the practicer still more in love with the fair act.

Anthony Ashley Cooper Shaftesbury

In nothing do men approach so nearly to the gods as in doing good to men.

Marcus Tullius Cicero

The best thing to give to your enemy is forgiveness; to an opponent, tolerance; to a friend, your heart; to your child, a good example; to a father, difference; to your mother, conduct that will make her proud of you; to yourself, respect; to all men, charity.

Francis Balfour

The place is dignified by the doer's deed.

William Shakespeare

There is a transcendent power in example. We reform others unconsciously when we walk uprightly.

Madame Swetchine

You need more tact in the dangerous art of giving than in any other social action.

William Bolitho

In this world it is not what we take up, but what we give up, that make us rich.

Henry Ward Beecher

There cannot be a more glorious object in creation than a human being replete with benevolence, meditating in what manner he may render himself most acceptable to the Creator by doing good to his creatures.

Henry Fielding

Life is not so short but that there is always time for courtesy.

Ralph Waldo Emerson

He only does not live in vain, who employs his wealth, his thought, [and] his speech to advance the good of others.

Hindu Maxim

To listen well, is as powerful as a means of influence as to talk well, and is as essential to all true conversation.

Author Unknown

It is not enough to help the feeble up, but to support him after.

William Shakespeare

A single conversation across the table with a wise man is worth a month's study of books.

Chinese Proverb

Liberality consists rather in giving seasonably than much.

Jean de la Bruyére

They who scatter with one hand, gather with two, not always in coin, but in kind. Nothing multiplies so much as kindness.

John Wray

It is the glory of the true religion that it inculcates and inspires a spirit of benevolence.—It is a religion of charity, which none other ever was.—Christ went about doing good; he set the example to his disciples, and they abounded in it.

Thomas Fuller

Almost always the most indigent are the most generous.

Leszinski Stanislas

To commiserate is sometimes more than to give, for money is external to a man's self, but he who bestows compassion communicates his own soul.

William Mountford

Better it is to the right conduct of life to consider what will be the end of a thing, than what is the beginning of it; for what promises fair at first, may prove ill, and what seems at first a disadvantage, may prove very advantageous.

William V. Wells

Every noble work is at first impossible.

Thomas Carlyle

Just in proportion as a man becomes good, divine, Christ-like, he passes out of the region of theorizing into the region of benevolent activities.—It is good to think well; it is divine to act well.

Horace Mann

Men spend their lives in the service of their passions, instead of employing their passions in the service of their life.

Sir Richard Steele

If any man is rich and powerful he comes under the law of God by which the higher branches must take the burnings of the sun, and shade those that are lower; by which the tall trees must protect the weak plants beneath them.

Henry Ward Beecher

How easy is it for one benevolent being to diffuse pleasure around him, and how truly is a kind heart a fountain of gladness, making everything in its vicinity to freshen into smiles.

Washington Irving

Every good act is charity. Your smiling in your brother's face, is charity; and exhortation of your fellow-man to vitruous deeds, is equal to alm-giving; your putting a wanderer in the right road, is charity; your assisting the blind, is charity; your removing stones, and thorns, and other obstructions from the road, is charity; your giving water to the thirsty, is charity. A man's true wealth thereafter, is the good he does in this world to his fellowman. When he dies, people will say, "What property has he left behind him?" But the angels will ask, "What good deeds has he sent before him?"

Mohomet (Mohammed)

To rejoice in another's prosperity, is to give content to your own lot; to mitigate another's grief, is to alleviate or dispel your own.

Tryon Edwards

Compliments are only lies in court clothes.
John Sterling

Next to ingratitude, the most painful thing to bear is gratitude.

Henry Ward Beecher

181

In all the affairs of life, social as well as political, courtesies of a small and trivial character are the ones which strike deepest to the grateful and appreciating heart.

Henry Clay

There is no outward sign of true courtesy that does not rest on a deep moral foundation.

Johann Wolfgang von Goethe

A man there was, and they called him mad; the more he gave, the more he had.

John Bunyan

Always vote for a principle, though you vote alone, and you may cherish the sweet reflection that your vote is never lost.

John Quincy Adams

The first ingredient in conversation is truth; the next, good sense; the third, good humor, and the fourth, wit.

Sir William Temple

It is good for us to think that no grace or blessing is truly ours till we are aware that God has blessed some one else with it through us.

Phillips Brooks

PEACE, CONTENTMENT, AND SATISFACTION

If one should give me a dish of sand, and tell me there were particles of iron in it, I might look for them with my eyes, and search for them with my clumsy fingers, and be unable to detect them; but let me take a magnet and sweep through it, and it draws to itself the almost invisible particles by the mere power of attraction. The unthankful heart, like my finger in the sand, discovers no mercies; but let the thankful heart sweep through the day, and as the magnet finds the iron, so it will find in every hour, some heavenly blessings, only the iron in God's sand is gold!

Henry Ward Beecher

One of the Godlike things of this world is the veneration done to human worth by the hearts of men.

Thomas Carlyle

A wise man will always be contented with his condition, and will live rather according to the precepts of virtue, than according to the customs of his country.

Antisthenes

Who is content with nothing possesses all things.

Nicolas Boileau

I never complained of my condition but once, said an old man—when my feet were bare, and I had not money to buy shoes; but I met a man without feet, and became contented.—Content can soothe, where'er by fortune placed; can rear a garden in the desert waste.

Henry Kirke White

Contentment is natural wealth, luxury is artificial poverty.

Socrates

The fountain of content must spring up in the mind; and he who has so little knowledge of human nature as to see happiness by changing anything but his own disposition, will waste his life in fruitless efforts, and multiply the griefs which he proposes to remove.

Samuel Johnson

I have learned, in whatever state I am, therewith to be content.

Philippians 4:11

Tranquil pleasures last the longest; we are not fitted to bear long the burden of great joys.

Christian Nestell Bovee

I am always content with what happens; for I know what God chooses is better than what I choose.

Epictetus

Resign every forbidden joy; restrain every wish that is not referred to God's will; banish all eager desires, all anxiety; desire only the will of God; seek him alone and supremely, and you will find peace.

Bishop Francis de S. Fenelon

My God, give me neither poverty nor riches, but whatsoever it may be thy will to give, give me, with it, a heart that knows humbly to acquiesce in what is thy will.

Gotthold

Learn to be pleased with everything; with wealth, so far as it makes us beneficial to others; with poverty, for not having much to care for; and with obscurity, for being unenvied.

Plutarch

Content has a kindly influence on the shoulder of man, in respect of every being to whom he stands related. It extinguishes all murmuring, repining, and ingratitude toward that Being who has allotted us our part out there to act in the world. It destroys all inordinate ambition; gives sweetness to the conversation, and serenity to all the thoughts; and if it does not bring riches, it does the same thing by banishing the desire of them.

Joseph Addison

God has two dwellings: one in heaven, and the other in a meek and thankful heart.

Izaak Walton

It is right to be contented with what we have, never with what we are.

Sir James Mackintosh

Peace is rarely denied to the peaceful.

Johann Christoph Friedrich von Schiller

Praise is the best auxiliary to prayer.—He who most bears in mind what has been done for him by God will be most emboldened to ask for fresh gifts from above.

Henry Melville

Among the smaller duties of life, I hardly know any one more important than that of not praising where praise is not due. Reputation is one of the prizes for which men contend: it produces more labor and more talent than twice the wealth of a country could ever rear up. It is the coin of genius, and it is the imperious duty of every man to bestow it with the most scrupulous justice and wisest economy.

Sydney Smith

Would you judge of the lawfulness or unlawfulness of pleasure, take this rule: whatever weakens your reason, impairs the tenderness of your conscience, obscures your sense of God, or takes off the relish of spiritual things; in short, whatever increases the strength and authority of your body over your mind, that is sin to you, however innocent it may be in itself.

Robert Southey

We lose the peace of years when we hunt after the rapture of moments.

Edward George Bulwer-Lytton

Contentment is a pearl of great price, and whoever procures it at the expense of ten thousand desires makes a wise and happy purchase.

George Balguy

The only permanent emotion of the inferior man is fear—fear of the unknown, the complex, the inexplicable.

Henry L. Mencken

That hat happy state of mind, so rarely possessed, in which we can say, "I have enough," is the highest attainment of philosophy. Happiness consists, not in possessing much, but in being content with what we possess. He who wants little always has enough.

Johann Georg Zimmerman

The more quietly and peaceably we all get on, the better—the better for ourselves—the better for our neighbors. In nine cases out of ten the wisest policy is, if a man cheats you, quit dealing with him; if he is abusive, quit his company; if he slanders you, take care to live so that nobody will believe him: no matter who he is, or how he misuses you, the wisest way is generally to let him alone; for there is nothing better than this cool, calm, quiet way of dealing with wrongs we meet with.

Author Unknown

I cannot help being happy. I've struggled against it but to no good. Apart from an odd five minutes here and there, I have been happy all my life. There is, I am well aware, no virtue whatever in this. It results from a combination of heredity, health, good fortune, and shallow intellect.

Arthur Marshall

The worship most acceptable to God, comes from a thankful and cheerful heart.

Plutarch

189

There is only one duty: that is to be happy.

Denis Diderot

All happiness is a work of art: the smallest error falsifies it, the slightest hesitation alters it, the least heaviness spoils it, the slightest stupidity brutalizes it.

Marguerite Yourcenar

The greatest happiness you can have is knowing that you do not necessarily require happiness.

William Saroyan

The world would be both better and brighter if we would dwell on the duty of happiness, as well as on the happiness of duty.

Sir John Lubbock

Happiness consists in being perfectly satisfied with what we have got and with what we haven't got. It is not how much we have, but how much we enjoy it, that makes happiness.

Charles Haddon Spurgeon

In vain do they talk of happiness who never subdued an impulse in obedience to a principle. He who never sacrificed a present to a future good, or a personal to a general one, can speak of happiness only as the blind do of colors.

Horace Mann

Service to a just cause rewards the worker with more real happiness and satisfaction than any other venture of life.

Carrie Chapman Catt

Set happiness before you as an end, no matter in what guise of wealth, or fame, or oblivion even, and you will not attain it.—But renounce it and seek the pleasure of God, and that instant is the birth of your own.

Arthur S. Hardy

Man's ultimate happiness lies not in this life.

Saint Thomas Aquinas

A search for a single, inclusive good is doomed to failure. Such happiness as life is capable of comes from the full participation of all our powers in the endeavor to wrest from each changing situation of experience its own full and unique meaning.

John Dewey

The strength and the happiness of a man consists in finding out the way in which God is going, and going in that way, too.

Henry Ward Beecher

What happiness is, the Bible alone shows clearly and certainly, and points out the way that leads to the attainment of it.—"In Cicero and Plato, and other such writers," says Augustine, "I meet with many things acutely said, and things that excite a certain warmth of emotions, but in none of them do I find these words, 'Come unto me, all ye that labor, and are heavy laden, and I will give you rest.'"

Samuel Taylor Coleridge

Happiness is the legitimate fruitage of love and service. It never comes and never can come by making it an end, and it is because so many persons mistake here and seek for it directly, instead of loving and serving God, and thus obtaining it, that there is so much dissatisfaction and sorrow.

Arthur S. Hardy

Seek happiness for its own sake, and you will not find it; seek for duty, and happiness will follow as the shadow comes with the sunshine.

Tryon Edwards

It is not the place, nor the condition, but the mind alone that can make any one happy or miserable.

Sir Roger L'Estrange

It is only a poor sort of happiness that could ever come by caring very much about our own narrow pleasures. We can only have the highest happiness, such as goes along with true greatness, by having wide thoughts and much feeling for the rest of the world as well as ourselves; and this sort of happiness often brings so much pain with it, that we can only tell it from pain by its being what we would choose before everything else, because our souls see it is good.

George Eliot

I am happy and content because I think I am.

Alain René Lesage

There is but one way to tranquillity of mind and happiness; let this, therefore, be always ready at hand with thee, both when thou wakest early in the morning, and all the day long, and when thou goest late to sleep, to account no external things thine own, but commit all these to God.

Epictetus

The belief that youth is the happiest time of life is founded on a fallacy. The happiest person is the person who thinks the most interesting thoughts, and we grow happier as we grow older.

William Lyon Phelps

True happiness renders men kind and sensible; and that happiness is always shared with others.

Charles de Secondat Montesquieu

There is in all of us an impediment to perfect happiness, namely, weariness of what we possess, and desire for what we have not.

Madame de Rieux

The chief secret of comfort lies in not suffering trifles to vex us, and in prudently cultivating our under-growth of small pleasures.

James Sharp

An act of goodness is of itself an act of happiness. No reward coming after the event can compare with the sweet reward that went with it.

Maurice Maeterlinck

There is one way of attaining what we may term, if not utter, at least mortal happiness; it is by a sincere and unrelaxing activity for the happiness of others.

Edward George Bulwer-Lytton

The common course of things is in favor of happiness.— Happiness is the rule, misery the exception.—Were the order reverse, our attention would be called to examples of health and competency, instead of disease and want.

William Paley

Happiness is a sunbeam which may pass through a thousand bosoms without losing a particle of its original ray; nay, when it strikes on a kindred heart, like the converged light on a mirror, it reflects itself with redoubled brightness.—It is not perfected till it is shared.

Jane Porter

Objects we ardently pursue bring little happiness when gained; most of our pleasures come from unexpected sources.

Herbert Spencer

The great high-road of human welfare and happiness lies along the highway of steadfast well-doing, and they who are the most persistent and work in the truest spirit, will invariably be the most successful.

Samuel Smiles

We ask God to forgive us for our evil thoughts and evil temper, but rarely, if ever, ask him to forgive us for our sadness.

Robert W. Dale

Happiness consists in activity.—Such is the constitution of our nature.—It is a running stream, and not a stagnant pool.

John Mason Good

I have now reigned above fifty years in victory or peace, beloved by my subjects, dreaded by my enemies, and respected by my allies. Riches and honors, power and pleasure, have waited on my call, nor does any earthly blessing appear to have been wanting to my felicity. In this situation, I have diligently numbered the days of pure and genuine happiness which have fallen to my lot; they amount to fourteen. O man, place not thy confidence in this present world!

Caliph of Cordova Abdaleahman

If I may speak of myself, my happy hours have far exceeded, and far exceed, the scanty numbers of the Caliph of Spain; and I shall not scruple to add, that many of them are due to the pleasing number of the composing of my history.

Edward Gibbon

Man is the merriest, the most joyous of all the species of creation.—Above and below him all are serious.

Joseph Addison

To pursue joy is to lose it. The only way to get it is to follow steadily the path of duty, without thinking of joy, and then, it comes most surely unsought, and we "being in the way," the angel of God, bright-haired Joy, is sure to meet us.

Alexander Maclaren

There are four varieties in society; the lovers, the ambitious, observers, and fools. The fools are the happiest.

Hippolyte A. Taine

Happy are the kings whose thrones are founded on their people's hearts.

Henry Ford

Here below is not the land of happiness; it is only the land of toil; and every joy which comes to us is only to strengthen us for some greater labor that is to succeed.

Immanuel Hermann Fichte

The happiness of life may be greatly increased by small courtesies in which there is no parade, whose voice is too still to tease, and which manifest themselves by tender and affectionate looks, and little kind acts of attention.

Lawrence Sterne

Grief should be the instructor of the wise: sorrow is knowledge; they who know the most must mourn the deepest o'er the fatal truth, the tree of knowledge is not that of life.

George Gordon Noel Byron

An effort made for the happiness of others lifts [us] above ourselves.

Lydia M. Child

He that hath so many and great causes of joy, and yet is in love with sorrow and peevishness, deserves to starve in the midst of plenty, and to want comfort while he is encircled with blessings.

Jeremy Taylor

A man that knows how to mix pleasures with business, is never entirely possessed by them; he either quits or resumes them at his will; and in the use he makes of them he rather finds a relaxation of mind than a dangerous charm that might corrupt him.

Charles de Saint Denis Evremond

Pleasure is very seldom found where it is sought. Our brightest blazes of gladness are commonly kindled by unexpected sparks.

Samuel Johnson

The morose man takes both narrow and selfish views of life and the world; he is either envious of the happiness of others, or denies its existence.

Charles Simmons

The most delicate, the most sensible of all pleasures, consists in promoting the pleasure of others.

Jean de la Bruyére

There is little pleasure in the world that is true and sincere beside the pleasure of doing our duty and doing good. I am sure no other is comparable to this.

John Tillotson

The purest pleasures lie within the circle of useful occupation.—Mere pleasure, sought outside of usefulness, is fraught with poison.

Henry Ward Beecher

The question, "Which is the happiest season of life," being referred to an aged man, he replied: "When spring comes, and in the soft air the buds are breaking on the trees, and they are covered with blossoms, I think, How beautiful is Spring! And when the summer comes, and covers the trees with its heavy foliage, and singing birds are among the branches, I think, How beautiful is Summer! When autumn loads them with golden fruit, and their leaves bear the gorgeous tint of frost, I think, How beautiful is Autumn! And when it is sere winter, and there is neither foliage nor fruit, then I look up through the leafless branches, as I never could until now, and see the stars shine."

Lucius Annaeus Seneca

The sweetest pleasures are those which do not exhaust hope.

Peter Gaston de Levis

None has more frequent conversations with disagreeable self than the man of pleasure; his enthusiasms are but few and transient; his appetites, like angry creditors, are continually making fruitless demands for what he is unable to pay; and the greater his former pleasures, the more strong his regret, the more impatient his expectations. A life of pleasure is, therefore, the most unpleasing life.

Oliver Goldsmith

The true felicity of life is to be free from anxieties and perturbations; to understand and do our duties to God and man, and to enjoy the present without any serious dependence on the future.

Lucius Annaeus Seneca

There is no greater fool than he who deliberately goes searching for pleasures. For every pleasure to which he habituates himself beyond those which God has put in the natural course of life, is a new fire kindled in his bones, which will burn his life-substance for fuel.

James M. Ludlow

Let us be sure that our delights exclude not the presence of God: we may please ourselves so long as we do not displease Him.

Thomas Adams

A life of pleasure makes even the strongest mind frivolous at last.

Edward George Bulwer-Lytton

Enjoy present pleasures in such a way as not to injure future ones.

Lucius Annaeus Seneca

He who can at all times sacrifice pleasure to duty approaches sublimity.

John Caspar Lavater

People should be guarded against temptation to unlawful pleasures by furnishing them the means of innocent ones. In every community there must be pleasures, relaxations, and means of agreeable excitement; and if innocents are not furnished, resort will be had to criminal. Man was made to enjoy as well as labor, and the state of society should be adapted to this principle of human nature.

William Ellery Channing

Pleasure is in general, dangerous and pernicious to virtue.— To be able, therefore, to furnish pleasure that is harmless and pure and unalloyed, is as great a power as man can possess.

Samuel Johnson

Most pleasures, like flowers, when gathered, die.

Edward Young

It is sad to think how few our pleasures really are, and for which we risk eternal good.

Gamaliel Bailey

A poor spirit is poorer than a poor purse.

Thomas Fuller

Cheerfulness is health; its opposite, melancholy, is disease.

Thomas C. Haliburton

When we borrow trouble, and look forward into the future and see what storms are coming, and distress ourselves before they come, as to how we shall avert them if they ever do come, we lose our proper trustfulness in God. When we torment ourselves with imaginary dangers, or trials, or reverses, we have already parted with that perfect love which casteth out fear.

Henry Ward Beecher

Human felicity is produced not so much by great pieces of good fortune that seldom happen, as by little advantages that occur every day.

Benjamin Franklin

It is as healthy to enjoy sentiment as to enjoy jam.

Gilbert K. Chesterton

One of the most useless of all things is to take a deal of trouble in providing against dangers that never come. How many toil to lay up riches which they never enjoy; to provide for exigencies that never happen; to prevent troubles that never come; sacrificing present comfort and enjoyment in guarding against the wants of a period they may never live to see.

William Jay

God is glorified, not by our groans but by our thanksgivings; and all good thought and good action claim a natural alliance with good cheer.

Edwin Percy Whipple

A cheerful temper joined with innocence will make beauty attractive, knowledge delightful, and wit good-natured. It will lighten sickness, poverty, and affliction; convert ignorance into an amiable simplicity, and render deformity itself agreeable.

Joseph Addison

To make pleasures pleasant shortens them.

Charles Buxton

Wondrous is the strength of cheerfulness, and its power of endurance—the cheerful man will do more in the same time, will do it better, will persevere in it longer than the sad or sullen.

Thomas Carlyle

Cheerfulness is as natural to the heart of a man in strong health, as color to his cheek; and wherever there is habitual gloom, there must be either bad air, unwholesome food, improperly severe labor, or erring habits of life.

John Ruskin

Laugh if you are wise.

Martial

Get into the habit of looking for the silver lining of the cloud, and, when you have found it, continue to look at it, rather than at the leaden gray in the middle. It will help you over many hard places.

A. A. Willitts

The first and last thing required of genius is the love of truth.

Johann Wolfgang von Goethe

If I can put one touch of a rosy sunset into the life of any man or woman, I shall feel that I have worked with God.

George MacDonald

Of all the evil spirits abroad in the world, insincerity is the most dangerous.

James A. Froude

The pleasures of the world are deceitful; they promise more than they give. They trouble us in seeking them, they do not satisfy us when possessing them, and they make us despair in losing them.

Madam de Lambert

A good laugh is sunshine in a house.

William Makepeace Thackeray

Every one must have felt that a cheerful friend is like a sunny day, which sheds its brightness on all around; and most of us can, as we choose, make of this world either a palace or a prison.

Sir John Lubbock

You find yourself refreshed by the presence of cheerful people.—Why not make earnest effort to confer that pleasure on others?—Half the battle is gained if you never allow yourself to say anything gloomy.

Lydia M. Child

To be happy, the temperament must be cheerful, not gloomy and melancholy.—A propensity to hope and joy, is real riches; one to fear and sorrow, is real poverty.

David Hume

Cheerfulness is a friend to grace; it puts the heart in tune to praise God, and so religion by proclaiming to the world, that we serve a good master.—Be serious, yet cheerful.—Rejoice in the Lord always.

Thomas Watson

I am persuaded that every time a man smiles, but much more when he laughs, it adds something to this fragment of life.

Lawrence Sterne

The horse-laugh indicates coarseness or brutality of character.

John Caspar Lavater

A light heart lives long.

William Shakespeare

Happiness is like manna; it is to be gathered in grains, and enjoyed every day. It will not keep; it cannot be accumulated; nor have we got to go out of ourselves or into remote places to gather it, since it has rained down from Heaven, at our very doors.

Author Unknown

Laughter is a most healthful exertion; it is one of the greatest helps to digestion with which I am acquainted; and the custom prevalent among our forefathers, of exciting it at table by jesters and buffoons, was founded on true medical principles.

Christoph Wilhelm Hufeland

Man is the only creature endowed with the power of laughter; is he not also the only one that deserves to be laughed at?

Lord Greville

Men show their character in nothing more clearly than by what they think laughable.

Johann Wolfgang von Goethe

How much lies in laughter: the cipher key, wherewith we decipher the whole man!

Thomas Carlyle

He, whose first emotion on the view of an excellent production is to undervalue it, will never have one of his own to show.

John Aiken

God made both tears and laughter, and both for kind purposes; for as laughter enables mirth and surprise to breathe freely, so tears enable sorrow to vent itself patiently. Tears hinder sorrow from becoming despair and madness.

J. H. Leigh Hunt

If we consider the frequent reliefs we receive from laughter, and how often it breaks the gloom which is apt to depress the mind, one would take care not to grow too wise for so great a pleasure of life.

Joseph Addison

Though laughter is looked upon by philosophers as the property of reason, the excess of it has always been considered the mark of folly.

Joseph Addison

Man could direct his ways by plain reason, and support his life by tasteless food, but God has given us wit, and flavor, and brightness, and laughter to enliven the days of man's pilgrimage.

Sydney Smith

The man who cannot laugh is not only fit for treasons, stratagems, and spoils; but his whole life is already a treason and a stratagem.

Thomas Carlyle

Happiness is in action, and every power is intended for action; human happiness, therefore, can only be complete as all the powers have their full and legitimate play.

David Thomas

No one is more profoundly sad than he who laughs too much.

Jean Paul Richter

Action may not always bring happiness; but there is no happiness without action.

Benjamin Disraeli

Frequent and loud laughter is the characteristic of folly and ill manners; it is the manner in which the mob express their silly joy at silly things, and which they call being merry.—In my mind there is nothing so ill-bred as audible laughter.

Philip Dormer Stanhope Chesterfield

The life that has grown up and developed without laughter, and without the sunny brightness which youth justly claims as its right, lacks buoyancy and elasticity, and becomes heavy and unsympathetic, if not harsh and morose.

G. S. Reany

Men of the noblest dispositions think themselves happiest when others share their happiness with them.

William Duncan

They that deserve nothing should be content with anything. Bless God for what you have, and trust God for what you want. If we cannot bring our condition to our mind, we must bring our mind to condition; if a man is not content in the state he is in, he will not be content in the state he would be in.

Erskine Mason

CONTRADICTION, PERSECUTION, AND OPPOSITION

To banish, imprison, plunder, starve, hang, and burn men for religion, is not the gospel of Christ, but the policy of the devil.—Christ never used anything that looked like force or violence but once, and that was to drive bad men out of the temple, not to drive them in.

John Jortin

If there be light, then there is darkness; if cold, then heat; if height, depth also; if solid, then fluid; hardness and softness; roughness and smoothness; calm and tempest; prosperity and adversity; life and death.

Pythagoras

It is something to sparkle among diamonds; but to shine among pebbles is neither credit nor value worth the pretending.

Sir William Temple

We must not contradict, but instruct him that contradicts us; for a madman is not cured by another running mad also.

Antisthenes

It is ridiculous for any man to criticize the works of another if he has not distinguished himself by his own performances.

Joseph Addison

Most controversies would soon be ended, if those engaged in them would first accurately define their terms and then adhere to their definitions.

Tryon Edwards

He who tells a lie is not sensible how great a task he undertakes; for he must be forced to invent twenty more to maintain one.

Alexander Pope

The way of the world is to praise dead saints and persecute living ones.

Nathaniel Howe

The fate of unborn millions will now depend, under God, on the courage and conduct of this army...We have, therefore, resolved to conquer or die.

George Washington

Power exercised with violence has seldom been of long duration, but temper and moderation generally produce permanence in all things.

Lucius Annaeus Seneca

For belief or practices in religion no man ought to be punished or molested by any outward force whatever.

John Milton

Whenever you see persecution, there is more than a probability that truth is on the persecuted side.

Bishop Hugh Latimer

To be alone is to be different; to be different is to be alone.

Suzanne Gordon

There is nothing more unreasonable, more inconsistent with the rights of human nature, more contrary to the spirit and precepts of the Christian religion, more iniquitous and unjust, more impolitic, than persecution.—It is against natural religion, against revealed religion, and against sound policy.

Lord Mansfield

The camomile, the more it is trodden on, the faster it grows.

William Shakespeare

Prosperity is no just scale; adversity is the only balance to weigh friends.

Plutarch

Wise men ne'er sit and wail their loss, but cheerily seek how to redress their harms.

William Shakespeare

He who strikes the first blow admits he's lost the argument.

Chinese Proverb

If you would not have affliction visit you twice, listen at once to what it teaches.

James Burgh

The gem cannot be polished without friction, nor man perfected without trials.

Chinese Proverb

The lessons we learn in sadness are those that abide.— Sorrow clarifies the mind, steadies it, forces it to weigh things correctly.—The soil moist with tears best feeds the seeds of truth.

Theodore T. Munger

Come then, affliction, if my Father wills, and be my frowning friend. A friend that frowns is better than a smiling enemy.

Anonymous

Affliction is not sent in vain from the good God who chastens those that he loves.

Robert Southey

Affliction comes to us all not to make us sad, but sober; not to make us sorry, but wise; not to make us despondent, but by its darkness to refresh us, as the night refreshes the day; not to impoverish, but to enrich us, as the plow enriches the field; to multiply our joy, as the seed, by planting, is multiplied a thousand-fold.

Henry Ward Beecher

Tears are often the telescope by which men see far into heaven.

Henry Ward Beecher

Genuine morality is preserved only in the school of adversity; a state of continuous prosperity may easily prove a quicksand to virtue.

Johann Christoph Friedrich von Schiller

How fast we learn in a day of sorrow! Scripture shines out in a new effulgence; every verse seems to contain a sunbeam, every promise stands out in illuminated splendor; things hard to be understood become in a moment plain.

Horatius Bonar

In all places, and in all times, those religionists who have believed too much, have been more inclined to violence and persecution than those who have believed too little.

Caleb C. Colton

Strength is born in the deep silence of long-suffering hearts; not amidst joy.

Felecia Hermans

God washes the eyes by tears until they can behold the invisible land where tears shall come no more.

Henry Ward Beecher

The aim of an argument or discussion should not bevictory, but progress.

Joseph Joubert

Affliction is the wholesome soil of virtue, where patience, honor, sweet humility, and calm fortitude, take root and strongly flourish.

David Mallet

There is such a difference between coming out of sorrow merely thankful for belief, and coming out of sorrow full of sympathy with, and trust in, Him who has released us.

Phillips Brooks

Adversity has the effect of eliciting talents which in prosperous circumstances would have lain dormant.

Horace

The good things of prosperity are to be wished; but the good things that belong to adversity are to be admired.

Lucius Annaeus Seneca

In this wild world, the fondest and the best are the most tried, most troubled, and distressed.

George Crabbe

He that can heroically endure adversity will bear prosperity with equal greatness of soul; for the mind that cannot be dejected by the former is not likely to be transported with the latter.

Henry Fielding

A smooth sea never made a skillful mariner, neither do uninterrupted prosperity and success qualify for usefulness and happiness. The storms of adversity, like those of the ocean, rouse the faculties and excite the invention, prudence, skill, and fortitude of the voyager. The martyrs of ancient times, in bracing their minds to outward calamities, acquired a loftiness of purpose and a moral heroism worth a lifetime of softness and security.

Anonymous

The Lord gets his best soldiers out of the highlands of affliction.

Charles Haddon Spurgeon

Prosperity is a great teacher; adversity is greater. Possession pampers the mind; privation trains and strengthens it.

William Hazlitt

As in nature, as in art, so in grace; it is rough treatment that gives souls, as well as stones, their lustre. The more the diamond is cut the brighter it sparkles; and in what seems hard dealing, there God has no end in view but to perfect his people.

Thomas Guthrie

Prosperity is too apt to prevent us from examining our conduct; but adversity leads us to think properly of our state, and so is most beneficial to us.

Samuel Johnson

Times of general calamity and confusion have ever been productive of the greatest minds. The purest ore is produced from the hottest furnace, and the brightest thunderbolt is elicited from the darkest storm.

Caleb C. Colton

He that has never known adversity is but half acquainted with others, or with himself. Constant success shows us but one side of the world. For, as it surrounds us with friends, who will tell us only our merits, so it silences those enemies from whom alone we can learn our defects.

Caleb C. Colton

The capacity of sorrow belongs to our grandeur; and the loftiest of our race are those who have had the profoundest griefs because they have had the profoundest sympathies.

Henry Giles

Adversity is the diamond dust Heaven polishes its jewels with.

Robert Leighton

213

WADE COOK'S POWER QUOTES

Alas! by some degree of woe, we every bliss must gain; the heart can ne'er a transport know that never feels a pain.

Lord Lyttleton

Sorrows are our best educators. A man can see further through a tear than a telescope.

Author Unknown

Whole years of joy glide unperceived away, while sorrow counts the minutes as they pass.

William Havard

They talk of short-lived pleasures: be it so; pain dies as quickly, and lets her weary prisoner go; the fiercest agonies have shortest reign.

William Cullen Bryant

Pain is the deepest thing we have in our nature, and union through pain and suffering has always seemed more real and holy than any other.

Arthur Henry Hallam

The true and noble way to kill a foe, is not to kill him; you, with kindness, may so change him that he shall cease to be a foe, and then he's slain.

Aleyn

Who hath not known ill fortune, never knew himself, or his own virtue.

David Mallet

Paradoxical as it may seem, God means not only to make us good, but to make us also happy, by sickness, disaster and disappointment.

Cyrus A. Bartol

To go to law is for two persons to kindle a fire, at their own cost, to warm others and singe themselves to cinders; and because they cannot agree as to what is truth and equity, they will both agree to unplume themselves that others may be decorated with their feathers.

Owen Feltham

A disputant no more cares for the truth than the sportsman for the hare.

Alexander Pope

Neither praise nor blame is the object of true criticism.—Justly to discriminate, firmly to establish, wisely to prescribe, and honestly to award—these are the true aims and duties of criticism.

William Gilmore Simms

MONEY, FORTUNE, AND DEBT

No blister draws sharper than interest on money.——It works day and night; in fair weather and foul.——It gnaws at a man's substance with invisible teeth.——It binds industry with its film, as a fly is bound with a spider's web.——Debt rolls a man over and over, binding him hand and foot, and letting him hang on the fatal mesh, till the long-legged interest devours him.—— One had better make his bed of thistles, than attempt to lie at ease upon interest.

Henry Ward Beecher

Debt is the secret foe of thrift, as vice and idleness are its open foes.—The debt-habit is the twin brother of poverty.

Theodore T. Munger

Think what you do when you run in debt; you give to another power over your liberty. If you cannot pay at the time, you will be ashamed to see your creditor; will be in fear when you speak to him; will make poor, pitiful, sneaking excuses, and by degrees come to lose your veracity, and sink into base, downright lying— for the second vice is lying, the first is running in debt. A freeborn man ought not to be ashamed nor afraid to see or speak to any man living, but poverty often deprives a man of all spirit and virtue. It is hard for an empty bag to stand upright.

Benjamin Franklin

The first step in debt is like the first step in falsehood, involving the necessity of going on in the same course, debt following debt, as lie follows lie.

Samuel Smiles

Paying off debts is, next to the grace of God, the best means of delivering you from a thousand temptations to vanity and sin.— Pay your debts, and you will not have wherewithal to buy costly toys or pernicious pleasures.—Pay your debts, and you will not have what to lose to a gamester.—Pay your debts, and you will of necessity abstain from many indulgences that war against the spirit and bring you into captivity to sin, and cannot fail to end in your utter destruction, both of soul and body.

Patrick Delany

Put not your trust in money, but put your money in trust.

Oliver Wendell Holmes

How few, like Daniel, have God and gold together.

Bishop Henry Montague Villiers

Make money your god, [and] it will plague you like the devil.

Henry Fielding

A man who owes a little can clear it off in a little time, and, if he is prudent, he will: whereas a man who, by negligence, owes a great deal, despairs of ever being able to pay, and therefore never looks into his accounts at all.

Philip Domer Stanhope Chesterfield

"Out of debt, out of danger," is, like many other proverbs, full of wisdom; but the word danger does not sufficiently express all that the warning demands.—For a state of debt and embarrassment is a state of positive misery, and the sufferer is as one haunted by an evil spirit, and his heart can know neither rest nor peace till it is cast out.

Charles Bridges

Compliments of congratulation are always kindly taken, and cost nothing but pen, ink, and paper. I consider them as draughts upon good breeding, where the exchange is always greatly in favor of the drawer.

Philip Dormer Stanhope Chesterfield

I have discovered the philosopher's stone, that turns everything into gold: it is, "Pay as you go."

John Randolph

A vain man's motto is: "Win gold and wear it;" a generous, "Win gold and share it;" a miser's, "Win gold and hoard it;" a profligate's, "Win gold and spend it;" a broker's, "Win gold and lend it;" a wise man's, "Win gold and use it."

Author Unknown

Lend not beyond thy ability, nor refuse to lend out of thy ability; especially when it will help others more than it can hurt thee. If thy debtor be honest and capable, thou hast thy money again, if not with increase, with praise. If he prove insolvent do not ruin him to get that which it will not ruin thee to lose; for thou art but a steward, and another is thy owner, master, and judge.

William Penn

Remember that money is of a prolific, generating nature. Money can beget money, and its offspring can beget more, and so on. Five shillings turned is six; turned again, it is seven; and so on till it becomes a hundred pounds. The more there is of it, the more it produces at every turning, so that the profits rise quicker and quicker. He that murders a crown, destroys all that it might have produced, even scores of pounds.

Benjamin Franklin

Money never made a man happy yet, nor will it. There is nothing in its nature to produce happiness. The more a man has, the more he wants. Instead of its filling a vacuum, it makes one. If it satisfies one want, it doubles and trebles that want another way. That was a true proverb of the wise man, rely upon it: "Better is little with the fear of the Lord, than great treasure, and trouble therewith."

Benjamin Franklin

Make all you can, save all you can, give all you can.
John Wesley

Refrain from covetousness, and thy estate shall prosper.

Plato

Gold, like the sun, which melts wax but hardens clay, expands great shoulders and contracts bad hearts.

Antoine Rivarol

Men are seldom more innocently employed than when they are honestly making money.

Samuel Johnson

Neither a borrower nor a lender be; for loan oft loses both itself and friend.

William Shakespeare

Run not into debt, either for wares sold, or money borrowed; be content to want things that are not of absolute necessity, rather than to run up the score: such a man pays at the latter end, a third part more than the principal, and is in perpetual servitude to his creditors; lives uncomfortably; is necessitated to increase his debts to stop his creditors' mouths; and many times falls into desperate courses.

Sir Matthew Hale

It is not money, as is sometimes said, but the love of money— the excessive, selfish, covetous love of money, that is the root of all evil.

Author Unknown

The covetous man heaps up riches, not to enjoy, but to have them; he starves himself in the midst of plenty; cheats and robs himself of that which is his own, and makes a hard shift to be as poor and miserable with a great estate as any man can be without it.

John Tillotson

It is much better to have your gold in the hand than in the heart.

Thomas Fuller

It is not from the tall, crowded workhouse of prosperity that men first or clearest see the eternal stars of heaven.

Theodore Parker

A man's ledger does not tell what he is, or what he is worth.—Count what is in man, not what is on him, if you would know what he is worth—whether rich or poor.

Henry Ward Beecher

It cannot be denied that outward accidents conduce much to fortune; favor, opportunity, death of others, occasion fitting virtue: but chiefly, the mold of a man's fortune is in his own hands.

Francis Bacon

As there is no worldly gain without some loss, so there is no worldly loss without some gain. If thou has lost thy wealth, thou has lost some trouble with it. If thou art degraded from thy honor, thou art likewise freed from the stroke of envy. If sickness hath blurred thy beauty, it has delivered thee from pride.—Set the allowance against the loss and thou shalt find no loss great. He loses little or nothing who reserves himself.

Francis Quarles

When wealth is lost, nothing is lost; when health is lost, something is lost; when character is lost, all is lost.

German Motto

Liberality consists rather in giving seasonably than much.

Jean de la Bruyére

We have comforts that kings might consider luxuries, yet it is real punishment for us to stay at home; we have wealth and occupation, but little of that piece of mind surpassing wealth which the sage finds in meditation.

Dr. Joseph Collins

Poverty is uncomfortable, as I can testify: but nine times out of ten the best thing that can happen to a young man is to be tossed overboard and compelled to sink or swim for himself.

James A. Garfield

Money is not required to buy one necessity of the soul.

Henry David Thoreau

Not to be able to bear poverty is a shameful thing; but not to know how to chase it away by work is a more shameful thing yet.

Pericles

Poverty is not dishonorable in itself, but only when it comes from idleness, intemperance, extravagance, and folly.

Plutarch

A castle after all is but a house—the dullest one when lacking company.

James Sheridan Knowles

The darkest hour in the history of any young man is when he sits down to study how to get money without honestly earning it.

Horace Greeley

Be busy in trading, receiving, and giving, for life is too good to be wasted in living.

John Sterling

Of all the advantages which come to any young man, I believe it to be demonstrably true that poverty is the greatest.

Josiah Gilbert Holland

In proportion as nations get more corrupt, more disgrace will attach to poverty, and more respect to wealth. There are two questions that would completely reverse this order of things: "What keeps some persons poor? and what has made others rich?" The true answer to these queries would often make the poor man more proud of his poverty than the rich man is of his wealth, and the rich man more justly ashamed of his wealth, than the poor man unjustly is of his poverty.

Caleb C. Colton

Our children, relations, friends, honors, houses, lands, and endowments, the goods of nature and fortune, nay, even of grace itself, are only lent. It is our misfortune, and our sin, to fancy they are given. We start, therefore, and are angry when the loan is called in. We think ourselves masters when we are only stewards, and forget that to each of us it will one day be said, "Give an account of thy stewardship."

Bishop George Horne

If you lend a person money it becomes lost for any purposes of your own.—When you ask for it back again, you find a friend made an enemy by your own kindness.—If you begin to press still further, either you must part with what you have lent or else you must lose your friend.

Plautus

If you would know the value of money, go and try to borrow some; for he that goes a-borrowing goes a-sorrowing.

Benjamin Franklin

All our money has a moral stamp. It is coined over again in an inward mint. The uses we put it to, the spirit in which we put it to, the spirit in which we spend it, give it a character which is plainly perceptible to the eye of God.

Thomas Starr King

A wise man should have money in his head, not in his heart.

Jonathan Swift

RIGHT ATTITUDES

All the performances of human art, at which we look with praise or wonder, are instances of the resistless force of perseverance: it is by this that the quarry becomes a pyramid, and that distant countries are united with canals. If a man was to compare the effect of a single stroke of the pick-ax, or of one impression of the spade with the general design and last result, he would be overwhelmed by the sense of their disproportion; yet those petty operations, incessantly continued, in time surmount the greatest difficulties, and mountains are levelled, and oceans bounded, by the slender force of human beings.

Samuel Johnson

Goodness is the only investment that never fails.

Henry David Thoreau

It is not the place that maketh the person, but the person that maketh the place honorable.

Marcus Tullius Cicero

We imitate only what we believe and admire.

Robert Aris Willmott

Insist on yourself; never imitate. Your own gift you can present every moment with the cumulative force of a whole life's cultivation; but of the adopted talent of another, you have only an extemporaneous half-possession. That which each can do best none but his Maker can teach him.

Ralph Waldo Emerson

Seek not goodness from without; seek it within yourselves, or you will never find it.

Epictetus

It is by imitation, far more than by precept, that we learn everything; and what we learn thus, we acquire not only more effectually, but more pleasantly.—This forms our manners, our opinions, our lives.

Edmund Burke

He who thinks his place below him, will certainly be below his place.

J. F. Saville

Precepts are useful, but practice and imitation go far beyond them.— Hence the importance of watching early habits that they may be free from what is objectionable.

Sir William Knighton

Greatness lies, not in being strong, but in the right using of strength; and strength is not used rightly when it serves only to carry a man above his fellows for his own solitary glory. He is the greatest whose strength carries up the most hearts by the attraction of his own.

Anonymous

There never was any heart truly great and gracious, that was not also tender and compassionate.

Robert South

Difficulty is a nurse of greatness—a harsh nurse, who rocks her foster children roughly, but rocks them into strength and athletic proportions.—The mind, grappling with great aims and wrestling with mighty impediments, grows by a certain necessity to the stature of greatness.

William Cullen Bryant

Great men are the commissioned guides of mankind, who rule their fellows because they are wiser.

Thomas Carlyle

The conditions of conquest are always easy. We have but to toil awhile, endure awhile, believe always, and never turn back.

William Gilmore Simms

Distinction is the consequence, never the object, of a great mind.

Washington Allston

There never was yet a truly great man that was not at the same time truly virtuous.

Benjamin Franklin

What do we live for, if it is not to make life less difficult to each other?

George Eliot

The theory that a great man is merely the product of his age, is rejected by the common observations of mankind.—The power that guides large masses of men, and shapes the channels in which the energies of a great people flow, is something more than a mere aggregate of derivative forces. It is a compound product, in which the genius of the man is one element, and the sphere opened to him by the character of his age and the institutions of his country, is another.

George Stillman Hillard

The reason why great men meet with so little pity or attachment in adversity would seem to be this: the friends of a great man were made by his fortune, his enemies by himself, and revenge is a much more punctual paymaster than gratitude.

Caleb C. Colton

Subtract from the great man all that he owes to opportunity, all that he owes to chance, and all that he has gained by the wisdom of his friends and the folly of his enemies, and the giant will often be seen to be a pigmy.

Caleb C. Colton

Perseverance gives power to weakness, and opens to poverty the world's wealth. It spreads fertility over the barren landscape, and bids the choicest fruits and flowers spring up and flourish in the desert abode of thorns and briers.

Samuel G. Goodrich

A grateful thought toward heaven is of itself a prayer.

Gotthold E. Lessing

Man is an imitative creature, and whoever is foremost leads the herd.

Johann Christoph Friedrich von Schiller

The virtue lies in the struggle, not in the prize.

Richard M. Milnes

If the title of great man ought to be reserved for him who cannot be charged with an indiscretion or a vice; who spent his life in establishing the independence, the glory, and durable prosperity of his country; who succeeded in all that he undertook, and whose successes were never won at the expense of honor, justice, integrity, or by the sacrifice of a single principle—this title will not be denied to Washington.

Jared Sparks

Great effects come of industry and perseverance; for audacity doth almost bind and mate the weaker sort of minds.

Francis Bacon

It is all very well to tell me that a young man has distinguished himself by a brilliant first speech. He may go on, or he may be satisfied with his first triumph; but show me a young man who has not succeeded at first, and nevertheless has gone on, and I will back that young man to do better than most of those who have succeeded at the first trial.

Charles James Fox

There is no royal road to anything.—One thing at a time, and all things in succession. That which grows slowly endures.

Josiah Gilbert Holland

Perseverance and audacity generally win.

Madame Dorothée Deluzy

It would be an unspeakable advantage, both to the public and private, if men would consider that great truth, that no man is wise or safe, but he that is honest.

Sir Walter Raleigh

A solemn and religious regard to spiritual and eternal things is an indispensable element of all true greatness.

Daniel Webster

There are two ways of attaining an important end—force and perseverance. Force falls to the lot only of the privileged few, but austere and sustained perseverance can be practiced by the most insignificant. Its silent power grows irresistible with time.

Madame Swetchine

I'm proof against that word failure. I've seen behind it. The only failure a man ought to fear is failure in cleaving to the purpose he sees to be best.

George Eliot

Victory belongs to the most persevering.

Napoleon Bonaparte

After listening to thousands of prayers for pardon to offenders, I can hardly recall a case where I did not feel that I might have fallen as my fellow-man has done, if I had been subjected to the same demoralizing influences and pressed by the same temptations.

Horatio Seymour

It is to be lamented that great characters are seldom without a blot.

George Washington

Humility is a virtue all preach, none practice, and yet everybody is content to hear. The master thinks it good doctrine for his servant, the laity for the clergy, and the clergy for the laity.

John Selden

Money dishonestly acquired is never worth its cost, while a good conscience never costs as much as it is worth.

Jean-Antoine Petit-Senn

As thou desirest the love of God and man, beware of pride. It is a tumor in the mind, that breaks and ruins all thine actions; a worm in thy treasury, that eats and ruins thine estate. It loves no man, and is beloved of none; it disparages another's virtues by detraction, and thine own by vainglory. It is the friend of the flatterer, the mother of envy, the nurse of fury, the sin of devils, the devil of mankind. It hates superiors, scorns inferiors, and owns no equal. In short, till thou hate it, God hates thee.

Author Unknown

Pride is not the heritage of man; humility should dwell with frailty, and atone for ignorance, error, and imperfection.

Sydney Smith

It is vain thought to flee from the work that God appoints us, for the sake of finding a greater blessing, instead of seeking it where alone it is to be found—in loving obedience.

George Eliot

I have been more and more convinced, the more I think of it, that, in general, pride is at the bottom of all great mistakes. All the other passions do occasional good; but whenever pride puts in its word, everything goes wrong; and what it might really be desirable to do, quickly and innocently, it is mortally dangerous to do proudly.

John Ruskin

True humility is not an abject, groveling, self-despising spirit; it is but a right estimate of ourselves as God sees us.

Tryon Edwards

He who imitates evil always goes beyond the example that is set; he who imitates what is good always falls short.

Francesco Guicciardini

Pride, like ambition, is sometimes virtuous and sometimes vicious, according to the character in which it is found, and the object to which it is directed. As a principle, it is the parent of almost every virtue and every vice—everything that pleases and displeases in mankind; and as the effects are so very different, nothing is more easy than to discover, even to ourselves, whether the pride that produces them is virtuous or vicious: the first object of virtuous pride is rectitude, and the next independence.

Lord Greville

There is this paradox in pride—it makes some men ridiculous, but prevents others from becoming so.

Caleb C. Colton

When flowers are full of heaven-descended dews, they always hang their heads; but men hold theirs the higher the more they receive, getting proud as they get full.

Henry Ward Beecher

Pride is the common forerunner of a fall. It was the devil's sin, and the devil's ruin; and has been, ever since, the devil's strategem, who, like an expert wrestler, usually gives a man a lift before he gives him a throw.

Robert South

It is not a great thing to be humble when you are brought low; but to be humble when you are praised is a great and rare attainment.

Saint Bernard

Patience is power; with time and patience the mulberry leaf becomes silk.

Chinese Proverb

Nature has given us pride to spare us the pain of being conscious of our imperfections.

Francois Duc de La Rochefoucauld

Principle is a passion for truth and right.

William Hazlitt

Obedience is the mother of success and is wedded to safety.

Aeschylus

How will you find good? It is not a thing of choice; it is a river that flows from the foot of the invisible throne, and flows by the path of obedience.

George Eliot

I pity the man who can travel from Dan to Beersheba, and cry, 'tis all barren—and so it is, and so is all the world to him who will not cultivate the fruits it offers.

Lawrence Sterne

It is the close observation of little things which is the secret of success in business, in art, in science, and in every pursuit in life. Human knowledge is but an accumulation of small facts, made by successive generations of men,—the little bits of knowledge and experience carefully treasured up and growing at length into a mighty pyramid.

Samuel Smiles

Each one sees what he carries in his heart.

Johann Wolfgang von Goethe

No man doth safely rule but he that hath learned gladly to obey.

Thomas á Kempis

Everything comes if a man will only wait.

Tancred

Beware the fury of a patient man.
John Dryden

Patience does not mean indifference. We may work and trust and wait, but we ought not to be idle or careless while waiting.

Author Unknown

Our real blessings often appear to us in the shape of pains, losses, and disappointments; but let us have patience, and we soon shall see them in their proper figures.

Joseph Addison

The two powers which in my opinion constitute a wise man are those of bearing and forbearing.

Epictetus

Patience strengthens the spirit, sweetens the temper, stifles anger, extinguishes envy, subdues pride, bridles the tongue, restrains the hand, and tramples upon temptations.

Bishop George Horne

Patience is not passive: on the contrary it is active; it is concentrated strength.

Author Unknown

Enter into the sublime patience of the Lord. Be charitable in view of it. God can afford to wait; why cannot we, since we have Him to fall back upon? Let patience have her perfect work, and bring forth her celestial fruits.

Author Unknown

Honesty is the best policy.
Benjamin Franklin

A patient, humble temper gathers blessings that are marred by the peevish, and overlooked by the aspiring.

Edwin Hubbell Chapin

A proud man is seldom a grateful man, for he never thinks he gets as much as he deserves.

Henry Ward Beecher

Patience is the art of hoping.

Luc de Clapiers Vauvenargues

It is wise to apply the refined oil of politeness to the mechanism of friendship.

Colette

They also serve who only stand and wait.

John Milton

A curtain lecture is worth all the sermons in the world for teaching the virtue of patience and long suffering.

Washington Irving

Patience is the courage of the conqueror, the strength of man against destiny—of the one against the world, and of the soul against matter.—Therefore it is the courage of the gospel; and its importance, in a social view and to races and institutions, cannot be too earnestly inculcated.

Edward George Bulwer-Lytton

Humility is the root, mother, nurse, foundation, and bond of all virtue.
Saint John Chrysostom

An ungrateful man is like a hog under a tree eating acorns, but never looks up to see where they come from.

Timothy Dexter

He that will not give some portion of his ease, his blood, his wealth, for others' good, is a poor, frozen churl.

Joanna Baillie

True politeness is perfect ease and freedom. It simply consists in treating others just as you love to be treated yourself.

Philip Dormer Stanhope Chesterfield

The last, best fruit which comes to late perfection, even in the kindliest soul, is tenderness toward the hard, forbearance toward the unforbearing, warmth of heart toward the cold, philanthropy toward the misanthropic.

Henri Richter

Wicked men obey from fear; good men, from love.

Aristotle

Discourtesy does not spring merely from one bad quality, but from several—from foolish vanity, from ignorance of what is due to others, from indolence, from stupidity, from distraction of thought, from contempt of others, from jealousy.

Jean de la Bruyére

Expedients are for the hour; principles for the ages.

Henry Ward Beecher

"Politeness," says Witherspoon, "is real kindness kindly expressed;" an admirable definition, and so brief that all may easily remember it. This is the sum and substance of all true politeness. Put it in practice, and all will be charmed with your manners.

Lydia H. Sigourney

A polite man is one who listens with interest to things he knows all about, when they are told him by a person who knows nothing about them.

Philippe de Mornay

There is no outward sign of politeness which has not a deep, moral reason. Behavior is a mirror in which every one shows his own image. There is a politeness of heart akin to love, from which springs the easiest politeness of outward behavior.

Author Unknown

Politeness is a mixture of discretion, civility, complaisance, and circumspection spread over all we do and say.

Charles de Saint Denis Evremond

The teeth are smiling, but is the heart?

Congolese Proverb

A good disposition is a virtue in itself, and it is lasting; the burden of the years cannot depress it, and love that is founded on it endures to the end.

Ovid

We all live in the hope of pleasing somebody; and the pleasure of pleasing ought to be greatest, and always will be greatest, when our endeavors are exerted in consequence of our duty.

Samuel Johnson

A word of kindness is seldom spoken in vain, while witty sayings are as easily lost as the pearls slipping from a broken string.

George D. Prentice

It is the witness still of excellence to put a strange face on its own perfection.
William Shakespeare

People who make a point of pleasing everybody seldom have a heart for any one. The love of self is the secret of their desire to please and their temper is generally fickle and insincere.

Charles Reade

"What is grace?" was asked of an old colored man who, for over forty years, had been a slave.—"Grace," he replied, "is what I should call giving something for nothing."

Author Unknown

There is no such way to attain to greater measure of grace as for a man to live up to the little grace he has.

James Gordon Brooks

As heat is opposed to cold, and light to darkness, so grace is opposed to sin.—Fire and water may as well agree in the same vessel, as grace and sin in the same heart.

Thomas Brooks

The being of grace must go before the increase of it; for there is no growth without life, and no building without a foundation.

George Lavington

Grace is but glory begun, and glory is but grace perfected.

Jonathan Edwards

Whatever is graceful is virtuous, and whatever is virtuous is graceful.

Marcus Tullius Cirero

A right judgment draws us a profit from all things we see.

William Shakespeare

God appoints our graces to be nurses to other men's weaknesses.

Henry Ward Beecher

Grace comes into the soul, as the morning sun into the world; first a dawning; then a light; and at last the sun in his full and excellent brightness.

Thomas Adams

Do all that you can to stand, and then fear lest you may fall, and by the grace of God you are safe.

William Penn

Our distinctions do not lie in the places we occupy, but in the grace and dignity with which we fill them.

William Gilmore Simms

Steady, patient, persevering thinking will generally surmount every obstacle in search after truth.

Nathaniel Emmons

Be patient in little things. Learn to bear the every-day trials and annoyances of life quietly and calmly, and then, when unforeseen trouble or calamity comes, your strength will not forsake you.

Author Unknown

As charity covers a multitude of sins before God, so does politeness before men.

Lord Greville

O Lord, who lends me life, lend me a heart replete with thankfulness.

William Shakespeare

Kindness in women, not their beauteous looks, shall win my love.

William Shakespeare

He that can have patience, can have what he will.

Benjamin Franklin

245

Good nature is worth more than knowledge, more than money, more than honor, to the persons who possess it.

Henry Ward Beecher

All that I have accomplished, or expect or hope to accomplish, has been and will be by that plodding, patient, persevering process of accretion which builds the ant-heap, particle by particle, thought by thought, fact by fact.

Elihu Burritt

LIFE
AND
DEATH

To live is not merely to breathe, it is to act; it is to make use of our organs, senses, faculties, of all those parts of ourselves which give us the feeling of existence. The man who has lived longest is not the man who has counted most years, but he who has enjoyed life most. Such a one was buried a hundred years old, but he was dead from his birth. He would have gained by dying young; at least he would have lived till that time.

Jean Jacques Rousseau

It is a modest creed, and yet
Pleasant if one considers it,
To own that death itself must be,
Like all the rest, a mockery.

Shelley

Dying is an art,
like everything else.
I do it exceptionally well.

Sylvia Plath

Most people die at the last minute; others twenty years before hand, some even earlier. They are the wretched of the earth.

Louis Ferdinand Céline

Life is thick sown with thorns, and I know no other remedy than to pass quickly through them. The longer we dwell on our misfortunes, the greater is their power to harm us.

Francois Marie de Voltaire

When I reflect, as I frequently do, upon the felicity I have enjoyed, I sometimes say to myself that, were the offer made me, I would engage to run again, from the beginning to end, the same career of life. All I would ask, should be the privilege of an author, to correct in a second edition, certain errors of the first.

Benjamin Franklin

A man should live with his superiors as he does with his fire; not too near, lest he burn; not too far off, lest he freeze.

Diogenes

We live in deeds, not years; in thoughts, not breaths; in feelings, not in figures on the dial; we should count time by heart-throbs. He most lives who thinks most, feels the noblest, acts the best.

Gamaliel Bailey

Life, if properly viewed in any aspect, is great, but mainly great when viewed in its relation to the world to come.

Albert Barnes

To complain that life has no joys while there is a single creature whom we can relieve by our bounty, assist by our counsels, or enliven by our presence, is to lament the loss of that which we possess, and is just as rational as to die of thirst with the cup in our hands.

Sir Thomas Fitzosborne

He who increases the endearments of life, increases at the same time the terrors of death.

Edward Young

Life, like every other blessing, derives its value from its use alone. Not for itself, but for a nobler end the eternal gave it; and that end is virtue.

Samuel Johnson

A sacred burden is this life ye bear; look on it; lift it; bear it solemnly; fail not for sorrow; falter not for sin; but onward, upward, till the goal ye win.

Frances Ann Kemble

Life is a journey, not a home; a road, not a city of habitation; and the enjoyments and blessings we have are but little inns on the roadside of life, where we may be refreshed for a moment, that we may with new strength press on to the end—to the rest that remaineth for the people of God.

Author Unknown

The truest end of life is to know the life that never ends.

William Penn

251

Live while you live, the epicure would say, and seize the pleasures of the passing day.—Live while you live, the sacred preacher cries, and give to God each moment as it flies.—Lord, in my views, let both united be. I live in pleasure while I live to thee.

Philip Doddridge

The most we can get out of life is its discipline for ourselves, and its usefulness for others.

Tryon Edwards

The shaping of our own life is our own work. It is a thing of beauty, or a thing of shame, as we ourselves make it. We lay the corner and add joint to joint, we give the proportion, we set the finish. It may be a thing of beauty and of joy for ever. God forgive us if we pervert our life from putting on its appointed glory!

Henry Ware

Yet through all, we know this tangled skein is in the hands of One who sees the end from the beginning; he shall yet unravel all.

Alexander Smith

Be such a man, and live such a life, that if every man were such as you, and every life a life like yours, this earth would be God's Paradise.

Phillips Brooks

The truest view of life has always seemed to me to be that which shows that we are here not to enjoy, but to learn.

Frederick William Robertson

A voice within us speaks that startling word, "Man, thou shalt never die!"— Celestial voices hymn it to our souls; according to harps, by angel fingers touched do sound forth still the song of our great immortality.

James Dwight Dana

Death is not to the Christian what is has often been called, "Paying the debt of nature;" it is rather bringing a note to the bank to obtain solid gold for it.—You bring a cumbrous body which is nothing worth, and lay it down, and receive for it, from the eternal treasures, liberty, victory, knowledge, and rapture.

John Foster

I congratulate you and myself, that life is passing fast away. What a superlatively grand and consoling idea is that of death! Without this radiant idea, life would, to my view, darken into midnight melancholy. Oh, the expectation of living here and living thus always would be indeed a prospect of overwhelming despair! But thanks be to that fatal decree that dooms us to die, and to that Gospel which opens the vision of an endless life; and thanks, above all, to that Saviour Friend who has promised to conduct all the faithful through the sacred trance of death, into scenes of paradise and everlasting delight!

John Foster

Live for something.—Do good, and leave behind you a monument of virtue that the storms of time can never destroy.— Write your name in kindness, love, and mercy on the hearts of thousands you come in contact with year by year, and you will never be forgotten.—Your name and your good deeds will shine as the stars of heaven.

Thomas Chalmers

On the imagination God sometimes paints, by dream and symbol, the likeness of things to come.—What the foolish-wise call fanaticism, belongs to the same part of us as hope.—Each is the yearning of the soul for the great "Beyond," which attests our immortality.

Edward George Bulwer-Lytton

The end of life is to be like God, and the soul following God will be like him.

Socrates

Death and the cross are the two great levellers; kings and their subjects, masters and slaves, find a common level in two places—at the foot of the cross, and in the silence of the grave.

Caleb C. Colton

It is impossible that anything so natural, so necessary, and so universal as death, should ever have been designed by Providence as an evil to mankind.

Jonathan Swift

A man really looking onward to an immortal life, on whatever grounds, exhibits to us the human soul in an ennobled attitude.

William Whewell

We do not believe in immortality because we have proved it, but we forever try to prove it because we believe it.

James Martineau

There appears to exist a greater desire to live long than to live well! Measure by man's desires, he cannot live long enough; measure by his good deeds, and he has not lived long enough; measure by his evil deeds, and he has lived too long.

Johann Georg Zimmerman

Every natural longing has its natural satisfaction.—If we thirst, God has created liquids to gratify thirst.—If we are susceptible of attachment, there are beings to gratify our love.—If we thirst for life and love eternal, it is likely that there are an eternal life and an eternal love to satisfy that craving.

Frederick William Robertson

Every man's life is a plan of God.

Horace Bushnell

What springs from earth dissolves to earth again, and heaven-born things fly to their native seat.

Marcus Antoninus

The life of every man is a diary in which he means to write one story, but writes another; and his humblest hour is when he compares the volume as it is with what he hoped to make it.

Sir James Matthew Barrie

'Tis the divinity that stirs within us; 'tis heaven itself that points out an hereafter and intimates eternity to man.

Joseph Addison

Lewdness is a very broad way to death, ornamented with artful flowers, and begins to allure and seduce travelers at an early age.—Parental watchfulness, guarding them from early childhood, should be diligent to keep them from this way to ruin.

Charles Simmons

One life; a little gleam of time between two eternities; no second chance for us forever more.

Thomas Carlyle

God gives to every man the virtue, temper, understanding, taste that lifts him into life, and lets him fall in just the niche he was ordained to fill.

Anonymous

Remember that life is neither pain nor pleasure; it is serious business, to be entered upon with courage and in a spirit of self-sacrifice.

Alexis Charles Henry de Tocqueville

Without duty, life is soft and boneless; it cannot hold itself together.

Joseph Joubert

Life will give you what you ask of her if only you ask long enough and plainly enough.

E. Nesbit

Life is rather a state of embryo, a preparation for life; a man is not completely born till he has passed through death.

Benjamin Franklin

Measure not life by the hopes and enjoyments of this world, but by the preparation it makes for another; looking forward to what you shall be rather than backward to what you have been.

Ludwig Tieck

How small a portion of our life it is that we really enjoy! In youth we are looking forward to things that are to come; in old age we are looking backward to things that are gone past; in manhood, although we appear indeed to be more occupied in things that are present, yet even that is too often absorbed in vague determinations to be vastly happy on some future day when we have time.

Caleb C. Colton

If I could get the ear of every young man for a few words, it would be this; make the most and best of yourself.—There is no tragedy like a wasted life—a life failing of its true end, and turned to a false end.

Theodore T. Munger

The Book of Life begins with a man and woman in a garden. It ends with Revelations.

Oscar Wilde

The hunger and thirst of immortality is upon the human soul, filling it with aspirations and desires for higher and better things than the world can give.—We can never be fully satisfied but in God.

Tryon Edwards

Use three physicians: first, Doctor Quiet; then, Dr. Merryman; and then, Doctor Diet.

Author Unknown

Some men are born old, and some never seem so. If we keep well and cheerful we are always young, and at last die in youth, even when years would count us old.

Tryon Edwards

The common man, who doesn't know what to do with his life, wants another which shall be endless.

Anatole France

There is room enough in human life to crowd almost every art and science in it. If we pass "no day without a line"—visit no place without the company of a book—we may with ease fill libraries, or empty them of their contents. The more we do, the more busy we are, the more leisure we have.

William Hazlitt

Consider the lilies of the field, whose bloom is brief.—We are as they; like them we fade away, as doth the leaf.

Constantine Rosetti

Such as thy words are, such will thy affections be esteemed; and such will thy deeds as thy affections, and such thy life as thy deeds.

Socrates

Life is a long lesson in humility.

Sir James Matthew Barrie

Life is the art of drawing sufficient conclusions from insufficient premises.

Samuel Butler

257

Nothing short of an eternity could enable men to imagine, think, and feel, and to express all they have imagined, thought and felt.—Immortality, which is the spiritual desire, is the intellectual necessity.

Edward George Bulwer-Lytton

The greatest results in life are usually attained by simple means and the exercise of ordinary qualities. These may for the most part be summed up in these two—common sense and perseverance.

Owen Feltham

EDUCATION, EXPERIENCE, AND STREET SMARTS

Studies serve for delight, for ornament, and for ability. Their chief use for delight is in privateness and retiring; for ornament is in discourse; and ability is in the judgment and disposition of business. For expert men can execute, and, perhaps, judge of particulars, one by one; but the general counsels and the plots and marshalling of affairs come best from those that are learned.

Francis Bacon

Do not be puffed up because of your knowledge nor overconfident because you are a learned person. Take counsel with the ignorant as well as the wise, for the limits of proficiency cannot be reached and no person is ever fully skilled.

Ptah-Hotep

The preservation of the means of knowledge among the lowest ranks is of more importance to the public than all the property of the rich men in the country.

John Quincy Adams

The superior man is he who develops, in harmonious proportions, his moral, intellectual, and physical nature.—This should be the end at which men of all classes should aim, and it is this only which constitutes real greatness.

Douglas Jerrold

Human nature is not a machine to be built after a model, and set to do exactly the work prescribed for it, but a tree, which requires to grow and develop itself on all sides, according to the tendency of the inward forces which make it a living thing.

John Stuart Mill

It is not proof of a man's understanding to be able to confirm whatever he pleases; but to be able to discern that what is true is true, and that what is false is false; this is the mark and character of intelligence.

Emanuel Swedenborg

I am indebted to my father for living, but to my teacher for living well.
Alexander of Macedon

It takes most men five years to recover from a college education, and to learn that poetry is as vital to thinking as knowledge.

Brooks Atkinson

A man cannot leave a better legacy to the world than a well-educated family.

Thomas Scott

We must despise no sort of talents; they all have their separate uses and duties; all have the happiness of man for their object; they all improve, exalt, and gladden life.

Sydney Smith

Human learning, with the blessing of God upon it, introduces us to divine wisdom; and while we study the works of nature, the God of nature will manifest himself to us; since, to a well-tutored mind, "The heavens declare his glory, and the firmament sheweth his handiwork."

Bishop George Horne

In the works of man as in those of nature, it is the intention which is chiefly worth studying.

Johann Wolfgang von Goethe

The true aim of every one who aspires to be a teacher should be, not to impart his own opinions, but to kindle minds.

Frederick William Robertson

The best teacher one can have is necessity.

Francois de La Noue

A wisely chosen illustration is almost essential to fasten the truth upon the ordinary mind, and no teacher can afford to neglect this part of his preparation.

Howard Crosby

Respect for the fragility and importance of an individual life is still the mark of the educated man.

Norman Cousins

Never explain. Your friends do not need it and your enemies will not believe you anyway.

Elbert Hubbard

Let no man value at a little price a virtuous woman's counsel.

George Chapman

Voracious learning, often over-fed, digests not into sense her motley meal. This bookcase, with dark booty almost burst, this forager on others' wisdom, leaves her native farm, her reason, quite untill'd.

Edward Young

Men give away nothing so liberally as their advice.

Francois Duc de La Rochefoucauld

Those who school others, oft should school themselves.

William Shakespeare

No man is so foolish but he may sometimes find another good counsel, and no man so wise that he may not easily err if he takes no other counsel than his own.—He that is taught only by himself has a fool for a master.

Ben Johnson

If I have made any improvement in the sciences, it is owing more to patient attention than to anything beside.

Sir Isaac Newton

Spirit is now a very fashionable word; to act with spirit, to speak with spirit, means only to act rashly, and to talk indiscreetly. An able man shows his spirit by gentle words and resolute actions; he is neither hot nor timid.

Phillip Dormer Stanhope Chesterfield

In composing, think much more of your matter than your manner. Spirit, grace, dignity of manner are of great importance, both to the speaker and the writer; but of infinitely more importance are the weight and worth of matter.

William W. Wirt

The highest function of the teacher consists not so much in imparting knowledge as in stimulating the pupil in its love and pursuit.

Henri Frederic Amiel

Every man, however wise, needs the advice of some sagacious friend in the affairs of life.

Plautus

It is a little learning, and but a little, which makes men conclude hastily.—Experience and humility teach modesty and fear.

Jeremy Taylor

Thoroughly to teach another is the best way to learn for yourself.

Tyron Edwards

Learn to say "No"; it will be of more use to you than to be able to read Latin.

Charles Haddon Spurgeon

To know how to suggest is the art of teaching.

Henri Frederic Amiel

A man should be careful never to tell tales of himself to his own disadvantage; people may be amused, and laugh at the time, but they will be remembered, and brought up against him upon some subsequent occasion.

Samuel Johnson

Attention makes the genius; all learning, fancy, science, and skill depend upon it.—Newton traced his great discoveries to it.—It builds bridges, opens new worlds, heals diseases, carries on the business of the world.—Without it, taste is useless, and the beauties of literature unobserved.

Robert Aris Willmott

It is the hardest thing in the world to be a good thinker without being a good self-examiner.

Anthony Ashley Cooper Shaftesbury

There are three classes of people in the world. The first learn from their own experience—these are wise; the second learn from the experience of others—these are the happy; the third neither learn from their own experience nor the experience of others— these are fools.

Anonymous

Seeing much, suffering much, and studying much, are the three pillars of learning.

Benjamin Disraeli

You are to consider that learning is of great use to society; and though it may not add to the stock, it is a necessary vehicle to transmit it to others. Learned men are the cisterns of knowledge, not the fountainhead.

James Northcote

That learning is most requisite which unlearns evil.

Antisthenes

A little learning is a dangerous thing! Drink deep, or taste not the Pierian spring; there shallow draughts intoxicate the brain, and drinking largely sobers us again.

Alexander Pope

Wear your learning, like your watch, in a private pocket.—Do not pull it out merely to show that you have one.—If asked what time it is, tell it; but do not proclaim it hourly and unasked, like the watchman.

Philip Dormer Stanhope Chesterfield

We should not ask who is the most learned, but who is the best learned.

Michel E. de Montaigne

He might have been a very clever man by nature, but he had laid so many books on his head that his brain could not move.

Robert Hall

All other knowledge is hurtful to him who has not the science of honesty and good nature.

Michel E. de Montaigne

Advice is seldom welcome. Those who need it most, like it least.

Samuel Johnson

It is easy to learn something about everything, but difficult to learn everything about anything.

Nathaniel Emmons

Some will never learn anything because they understand everything too soon.

Sir Thomas Pope Blount

Learning gives us a fuller conviction of the imperfections of our nature; which one would think, might dispose us to modesty: for the more a man knows, the more he discovers his ignorance.

Jeremy Collier

There is no study that is not capable of delighting us after a little application to it.

Alexander Pope

They are not the best students who are most dependent on books. What can be got out of them is at best only material; a man must build his house for himself.

George MacDonald

The man who has acquired the habit of study, though for only one hour every day in the year, and keeps to the one thing studied till it is mastered, will be startled to see the progress he has made at the end of a twelvemonth.

Edward George Bulwer-Lytton

Since I began to ask God's blessing on my studies, I have done more in one week than I have done in a whole year before.

Edward Payson

The more we study
the more we discover
our ignorance.

Percy Bysshe Shelley

We may divide thinkers into those who think for themselves, and those who think through others. The latter are the rule, and the former the exception. The first are original thinkers in a double sense, and egotists in the noblest meaning of the word. It is from them only that the world learns wisdom. For only the light which we have kindled in ourselves can illuminate others.

Arthur Schopenhauer

The love of study, a passion which derives fresh vigor from enjoyment, supplies each day and hour with a perpetual source of independent and rational pleasure.

Edward Gibson

To the man who studies to gain a thorough insight into science, books and study are merely the steps of the ladder by which he climbs to the summit; as soon as a step has been advanced he leaves it behind. The majority of mankind, however, who study to fill their memory with facts do not use the steps of the ladder to mount upward, but take them off and lay them on their shoulders in order that they may take them along, delighting in the weight of the burden they are carrying. They ever remain below because they carry what should carry them.

Arthur Schopenhauer

He who always seeks more light the more he finds, and finds more the more he seeks, is one of the few happy mortals who take and give in every point of time. The tide and ebb of giving and receiving is the sum of human happiness, which he alone enjoys who always wishes to acquire new knowledge, and always finds it.

John Caspar Lavater

One never learns by success. Success is the plateau that one rests upon to take breath and look down from upon the straight and difficult path, but one does not climb upon a plateau.

Josephone Preston Peabody

When God would educate a man He compels him to learn bitter lessons. He sends him to school to the necessities rather than to the graces, that, by knowing all suffering, he may know also the eternal consolation.

Celia Burleigh

Studies teach not their own use; that is a wisdom without them and above them, won by observation.

Francis Bacon

Discourses on morality and reflection on human nature, are the best means we can make use of to improve our minds, gain a true knowledge of ourselves, and recover our souls out of the vice, ignorance, and prejudice which naturally cleave to them.

Joseph Addison

The true grandeur of humanity is in moral elevation, sustained, enlightened and decorated by the intellect of man.

Charles Sumner

From the time when the exercise of intellect became the source of strength and wealth, every addition to science, every fresh truth, and every new idea became a germ of power placed within reach of the people.

Alexis Charles Henry de Tocqueville

He is a benefactor of mankind who contracts the great rules of life into short sentences, that may be easily impressed on the memory, and so recur habitually to the mind.

Samuel Johnson

Omit a few of the most abstruse sciences, and mankind's study of man occupies nearly the whole field of literature. The burden of history is what man has been; of law, what he does; of physiology, what he is; of ethics, what he ought to be; of revelation, what he shall be.

George Finlayson

Few things are harder to put up with than the annoyance of a good example.

Mark Twain

The divine insanity of noble minds, that never falters nor abates, but labors, endures, and waits, till all that it foresees it finds, or what it cannot find, creates.

Henry Wadsworth Longfellow

Man himself is the crowning wonder of creation; the study of his nature the noblest study the world affords.

William E. Gladstone

To be proud of learning is the greatest ignorance.

Jeremy Taylor

People seldom improve when they have no model but themselves to copy after.

Oliver Goldsmith

The common people do not accurately adapt their thoughts to objects; nor, secondly, do they accurately adapt their words to their thoughts; they do not mean to lie; but, taking no pains to be exact, they give you very false accounts. A great part of their language is proverbial; if anything rocks at all, they say it rocks like a cradle; and in this way they go on.

Samuel Johnson

People never improve unless they look to some standard or example higher and better than themselves.

Tryon Edwards

Every great advance in natural knowledge has involved the absolute rejection of authority.

Thomas H. Huxley

It is well to learn caution by the misfortunes of others.

Publius Syrus

A scholar knows no boredom.

Jean Paul Richter

To accept good advice is but to increase one's own ability.
Johann Wolfgang von Goethe

This is one of the sad conditions of life, that experience is not transmissible. No man will learn from the suffering of another; he must suffer himself. Every failure is a step to success; every detection of what is false directs us toward what is true; every trial exhausts some tempting form of error. Not only so, but scarcely any attempt is entirely a failure; scarcely any theory, the result of steady thought, is altogether false; no tempting form of error is without some latent charm derived from truth.

William Whewell

Experience is not what happens to you; it is what you do with what happens to you.

Aldous Huxley

Perfection does not exist; to understand it is the triumph of human intelligence; to expect to possess it is the most dangerous kind of madness.

Alfred de Musset

He who has no inclination to learn more will be very apt to think that he knows enough.

Thomas Powell

Study the past if you would divine the future.

Confucius

"Cogito ergo sum."

René Descartes

To behold is not necessarily to observe, and the power of comparing and combining is only to be obtained by education. It is much to be regretted that habits of exact observation are not cultivated in our schools, to this deficiency may be traced much of the fallacious reasoning and the false philosophy which prevails.

Karl Wilhelm Humboldt

Justice without wisdom is impossible.

James A. Froude

A man's genius is always, in the beginning of life, as much unknown to himself as to others; and it is only after frequent trials, attended with success, that he dares think himself equal to those undertakings in which those who have succeeded have fixed the admiration of mankind.

David Hume

Judgment is forced upon us by experience.

Samuel Johnson

Experience is the Lord's school, and they who are taught by Him usually learn by the mistakes they make that in themselves have no wisdom; and by their slips and falls, they have no strength.

John Newton

Experience keeps a dear school; but fools will learn in no other, and scarce in that; for it is true, we may give advice but we cannot give conduct.

Benjamin Franklin

Experience is a jewel, and it had need be so, for it is often purchased at an infinite rate.

William Shakespeare

It is good to rub and polish our brain against that of others.
Michel E. de Montaigne

Experience takes dreadfully high school wages, but he teaches like no other.

Thomas Carlyle

Experience is the common schoolhouse of fools and ill men.—Men of wit and honesty are otherwise instructed.

Desiderius Erasmus

Experience teaches slowly, and at the cost of mistakes.

James A. Froude

You cannot create experience, you undergo it.

Albert Camus

The highest purpose of intellectual cultivation is, to give a man a perfect knowledge and mastery of his own inner self.

Novalis

The knowledge of the world is only to be acquired in the world and not in a closet.

Philip Dormer Stanhope Chesterfield

A maxim is the exact and noble expression of an important and indisputable truth.—Sound maxims are the germs of good, strongly imprinted on the memory they fortify and strengthen the will.

Joseph Joubert

However learned or eloquent, man knows nothing truly that he has not learned from experience.

Christopher Martin Wieland

There are but few proverbial sayings that are not true, for they are all drawn from experience itself, which is the mother of all sciences.

Saavedra M. de Cervantes

He hazardeth much who depends for his learning on experience.—An unhappy master is he who is made wise only by many shipwrecks; a miserable merchant, who is neither rich nor wise till he has been bankrupt.—By experience we find out a short way instead of a long wandering.

Roger Ascham

Education begins the gentleman, but reading, good company, and reflection must finish him.

John Locke

Conversation enriches the understanding, but solitude is the school of genius.

Edward Gibbon

Experience is the name men give to their follies or their sorrows.

Alfred de Musset

It may serve as a comfort to us in all our calamities and afflictions, that he who loses anything and gets wisdom by it, is a gainer by the loss.

Sir Roger L'Estrange

The rules which experience suggests are better than those which theorists elaborate in their libraries.

Richard Salter Storrs

WADE COOK'S POWER QUOTES

They talk most who have the least to say.

Matthew Prior

It is a maxim received in life that, in general, we can determine more wisely for others than for ourselves.—The reason of it is so clear in argument that it hardly wants the confirmation of experience.

Junius

Experience is a hard teacher because she gives the test first, the lesson after.

Vernon Law

LITTLE THINGS MAKE A BIG DIFFERENCE

In dwelling on divine mysteries, keep thy heart humble, thy thoughts reverent, thy soul holy. Let not philosophy be ashamed to be confuted, nor logic to be confounded, nor reason to be surpassed. What thou canst not prove, approve; what thou canst not comprehend, believe; what thou canst believe, admire and love and obey. So shall thine ignorance be satisfied in thy faith, and thy doubt be swallowed up in thy reverence, and thy faith be as influential as sight. Put out thine own candle, and then shalt thou see clearly the sun of righteousness.

Jeremy Taylor

Minute events are the hinges on which magnificent results turn.—In a watch the smallest link, chain, ratchet, cog, or crank, is as essential as the main spring itself.—If one falls out the whole will stand still.

John Cumming

Little drops of water,
little grains of sand,
make the mighty ocean
and the pleasant land;
so the little minutes,
humble though they be,
make the mighty ages
of eternity.

Julia A. Fletcher Carney

The greatest things ever done on earth have been done by little and little—little agents, little persons, little things, by every one doing his own work, filling his own sphere, holding his own post, and saying, "Lord, what wilt thou have me to do?

Thomas Guthrie

A little more patience, a little more charity for all, a little more devotion, a little more love; with less bowing down to the past, and a silent ignoring of pretended authority; brave looking forward to the future with more faith in our fellows, and the race will be ripe for a great burst of light and life.

Elbert Hubbard

A little nonsense, now and then, is relished by the wisest men.

Anonymous

I was always an early riser. Happy the man who is! Every morning day comes to him with a virgin's love, full of bloom and freshness. The youth of nature is contagious, like the gladness of a happy child.

Edward George Bulwer-Lytton

The morning, pouring everywhere, its golden glory on the air.

Henry Wadsworth Longfellow

The power of little things has so often been noted that we accept it as an axiom, and yet fail to see, in each beginning, the possibility of great events.

F. P. Edwards

Most of the critical things in life, which become the starting points of human destiny, are the little things.

Robert P. Smith

The million little things that drop into our hands, the small opportunities each day brings. He leaves us free to use or abuse and goes unchanging along His silent way.

Helen Keller

There is no trifling with nature; it is always true, grave, and severe; it is always in the right, and the faults and errors fall to our share. It defies incompetency, but reveals its secrets to the competent, the truthful, and the pure.

Johann Wolfgang von Goethe

Do little things now; so shall big things come to thee by and by asking to be done.

Persian Proverb

The heavens themselves, the planets, and this centre, observe degree, priority and place, insisture, course, proportion, season, form, office, and custom, in all line of order.

William Shakespeare

There is nothing too little for so little a creature as man.—It is by studying little things that we attain the great art of having as little misery and as much happiness as possible.

Samuel Johnson

Life is made up, not of great sacrifices or duties, but of little things, in which smiles and kindness and small obligations, given habitually, are what win and preserve the heart and secure comfort.

Sir Humphrey Davy

But mighty nature bounds as from her birth:
the sun is in the heavens, and life on earth;
flowers in the valley, splendor in the beam,
health on the gale, and freshness in the stream.

George Gordon Noel Byron

Have a time and place for everything, and do everything in its time and place, and you will not only accomplish more, but have far more leisure than those who are always hurrying, as if vainly attempting to overtake time that had been lost.

Tryon Edwards

Most persons would succeed in small things if they were not troubled with great ambitions.

Henry Wadsworth Longfellow

Give me a positive character, with a positive faith, positive opinions and positive actions, though frequently in error, rather than a negative character, with a doubting faith, wavering opinions, undecided actions and faintness of heart. Something is better than nothing.

Charles Simmons

The morning itself, few inhabitants of cities know anything about. Among all our good people, not one in a thousand sees the sun rise once in a year. They know nothing of the morning. Their idea of it is that it is that part of the day which comes along after a cup of coffee and a piece of toast. With them, morning is not a new issuing of light, a new bursting forth of the sun, a new waking-up of all that has life from a sort of temporary death, to behold again the works of God, the heavens and earth; it is only a part of the domestic day, belonging to reading newspapers, answering notes, sending the children to school, and giving orders for dinner. The first streak of light, the earliest purpling of the east, which the lark springs up to greet, and the deeper, and deeper coloring into orange and red, till at length the "glorious sun is seen, regent of the day"—this they never enjoy, for they never see it. I never thought that Adam had much the advantage of us from having seen the world while it was new. The manifestations of the power of God, like his mercies, are "new every morning" and fresh every moment. We see as fine risings of the sun as ever Adam saw; and its risings are as much a miracle now as they were in his day— and, I think, a good deal more, because it is now a part of the miracle, that for thousands and thousands of years he has come to his appointed time, without the variation of a millionth part of a second. I know the morning—I am acquainted with it, and I love it. I love it fresh and sweet as it is—a daily new creation, breaking forth and calling all that have life and breath and being a new adoration, new enjoyments, and new gratitude.

Daniel Webster

Set all things in their own peculiar place, and know that order is the greatest grace.

John Dryden

He who has no taste for order, will be often wrong in his judgment, and seldom considerate or conscientious in his actions.

John Caspar Lavater

Good order is the foundation of all good things.

Edmund Burke

I follow nature as the surest guide, and resign myself, with implicit obedience, to her sacred ordinances.

Marcus Tullius Cicero

Order is the sanity of the mind, the health of the body, the peace of the city, the security of the state.—As the beams to a house, as the bones to the body, so is order to all things.

Robert Southey

Order means light and peace, inward liberty and free command over one's self; order is power.

Henri Frederic Amiel

Look, what envious streaks do lace the severing clouds in yonder east! Night's candles are burnt out, and jocund day stands tip-toe on the misty mountain-tops.

William Shakespeare

Other parts of the body assist the speaker but the hands speak themselves.—By them we ask, promise, invoke, dismiss, threaten, entreat, deprecate.—By them we express fear, joy, grief, our doubts, assent, or penitence; we show moderation or profusion, and mark number and time.

Quintilian

Let the day have a blessed baptism by giving your first waking thoughts into the bosom of God.—The first hour of the morning is the rudder of the day.

Henry Ward Beecher

I do not explain—I only state it; and this is all we can do with a large proportion of all the facts and truths that we know.— There is a point, easily reached, where the simplest facts end in mystery, even as they begin in it; just as each day lies between two nights.

Robert James Turnbull

Nature is the living, visible garment of God.

Johann Wolfgang von Goethe

Order is heaven's first law.

Alexander Pope

As defect of strength in us makes some weights to be immovable, so likewise, defect of understanding makes some truths to be mysterious.

Bishop Thomas Sherlock

The flower that follows the sun does so even in cloudy days.

Robert Leighton

...A man who thinks twice before saying nothing.

Frederick Sawyer

A great leader is a person who can tell you to go to hell in such a way that you actually look forward to the trip.

Caskie Stinett

Habit is stronger than reason.

George Santayana

Certainly, this is a duty—not a sin.—Cleanliness is, indeed, next to Godliness.

John Wesley

Live this day as if it were the last.

Alexander Kerr

A runaway monk never speaks well of his monastery.

Italian Proverb

A good conscience is a continual Christmas.

Benjamin Franklin

A compliment is usually accompanied with a bow, as if to beg pardon for paying it.

August W. Hare

A fool, indeed, has great need of a title; it teaches men to call him count or duke, and thus forget his proper name of fool.

John Crowne

There is only one thing in the world worse than being talked about, and that is not being talked about.

Oscar Wilde

Compliments which we think are deserved, we accept only as debts, with indifference; but those which conscience informs us we do not merit, we receive with the same gratitude that we do favors given away.

Oliver Goldsmith

A place for everything, everything in its place.

Benjamin Franklin

Beware of him that is slow to anger; for when it is long coming, it is the stronger when it comes, and the longer kept.—Abused patience turns to fury.

Francis Quarles

Despise not small things, either for evil or good, for a look may work thy ruin, or a word create thy wealth.—A spark is a little thing, yet it may kindle the world.

Martin Farquhar Tupper

Did I contradict myself? Very well then I contradict myself. (I am large, I contain multitudes.)

Walt Whitman

Thoughtfulness for others, generosity, modesty, and self-respect are the qualities which make a real gentleman or lady.

Thomas H. Huxley

The passions act as winds to propel our vessel, our reason is the pilot that steers her; without the winds she would not move; without the pilot she would be lost.

F. Schulz

A deserved and discriminating compliment is often one of the strongest encouragements and incentives to the diffident and self-distrustful.

Tryon Edwards

A truly elegant taste is generally accompanied with excellency of heart.

Henry Fielding

Days of respite are golden days.

Robert South

Taste is not stationary. It grows every day, and is improved by cultivation, as a good temper is refined by religion.

Robert Aris Willmott

It is the passions of men that both do and undo everything.— They are the winds that are necessary to put every thing in motion, though they often cause storms.

Bernard le B. de Fontenelle

The passions and capacities of our nature are foundations of power, happiness and glory; but if we turn them into occasions and sources of self-indulgence, the structure itself falls, and buries everything in its overwhelming desolation.

George B. Cheever

Hope springs eternal
in the human breast;
man never is, but
always to be blest.

Alexander Pope

The passions are like fire, useful in a thousand ways and dangerous only in one, through their excesses.

Christian Nestell Bovee

One hour's sleep before midnight, is worth two after.

Henry Fielding

Custom adapts itself to expediency.

Tactitus

To murder character is as truly a crime as to murder the body; the tongue of the slanderer is brother to the dagger of the assassin.

Tryon Edwards

Happy is he who is engaged in controversy with his own passions, and comes off superior; who makes it his endeavor that his follies and weaknesses may die before himself, and who daily meditates on mortality and immortality.

John Jortin

Hill and valley, seas and constellations, are but stereotypes of divine ideas appealing to, and answered by the living soul of man.

Edwin Hubbell Chapin

The laws of nature are the rules according to which effects are produced; but there must be a lawgiver—a cause which operates according to these rules.—The laws of navigation never steered a ship, and the law of gravity never moved a planet.

Thomas Reid

That which is striking and beautiful is not always good; but that which is good is always beautiful.

Ninon de L'Enclos

Surely, if all the world was made for man, then man was made for more than the world.

Pierre Alexandre Duplessis

Spare minutes are the gold-dust of time; the portions of life most fruitful in good or evil; the gaps through which temptations enter.

Anonymous

Alas! too well, too well they know the pain, the penitence, the woe, that passion brings down on the best, the wisest, and the loveliest.

Sir Thomas Moore

Half dust, half deity, alike unfit to sink or soar.
George Gordon Noel Byron

Remember that the most beautiful things in the world are the most useless; peacocks and lilies for instance.

John Ruskin

The criterion of true beauty is, that it increases on examination; if false, that it lessens.—There is therefore, something in true beauty that corresponds with right reason, and is not the mere creation of fancy.

Lord Greville

We deny the doctrine of the ancient Epicureans, that pleasure is the supreme good; of Hobbes, that moral rules are only the work of men's mutual fear; of Paley, that what is expedient is right, and that there is no difference among pleasures except their intensity and duration; and of Bentham, that the rules of human action are to be obtained by counting up the pleasures which actions produce.—And we maintain with Plato, that reason has a natural and rightful authority over desire and affection; with Butler, that there is a difference of kind in our principles of action; and with the general voice of mankind, that we must do what is right at whatever cost of pain and loss.—And why? Because it was right.

William Whewell

The cynic is one who never sees a good quality in a man, and never fails to see a bad one.—He is the human owl, vigilant in darkness and blind to light, mousing for vermin, and never seeing noble game.

Henry Ward Beecher

You cannot put a great hope into a small soul.

Jenkin Lloyd Jones

Heat water to the highest degree, you cannot make wine of it; it is water still; so, let morality be raised to the highest, it is nature still; it is old Adam put in a better dress.

Thomas Watson

To have known one good old man—one man who, through the chances and mischances of a long life, has carried his heart in his hand, like a palm branch, waving all discords into peace—helps our faith in God, in ourselves, and in each other, more than many sermons.

George William Curtis

A propensity to hope and joy is real riches; one to fear and sorrow, real poverty.

David Hume

The cares of today are seldom those of tomorrow; and when we lie down at night we may safely say to most of our troubles, "Ye have done your worst, and we shall see you no more."

William Cowper

It is an old saying, that charity begins at home; but this is no reason it should not go abroad; a man should live with the world as a citizen of the world; he may have a preference for the particular quarter or square, or even alley in which he lives, but he should have a generous feeling for the welfare of the whole.

Richard Cumberland

It is with narrow-souled people as with narrow-necked bottles; the less they have in them, the more noise they make in pouring it out.

Alexander Pope

MUSIC AND LIFE

There is something marvelous in music. I might almost say it is, in itself, a marvel. Its position is somewhere between the region of thought and that of phenomena; a glimmering medium between mind and matter, related to both and yet differing from either. Spiritual, and yet requiring rhythm; material, and yet independent of space.

Heinrich Heine

Music is the mediator between the spiritual and the sensual life. Although the spirit be not master of that which it creates through music, yet it is blessed in this creation, which, like every creation of art, is mightier than the artist.

Ludwig van Beethoven

Music is the harmonious voice of creation; an echo of the invisible world; one not of the divine concord which the entire universe is destined one day to sound.

Giuseppe Mazzini

Music resembles poetry; in each are numerous graces which no methods teach, and which a master hand alone can reach.

Alexander Pope

Explain it as we may, a martial strain will urge a man into the front rank of battle sooner than an argument, and a fine anthem excite his devotion more certainly than a logical discourse.

Henry Theodore Tuckerman

Where painting is weakest, namely, in the expression of the highest moral and spiritual ideas, there music is sublimely strong.

Harriet Beecher Stowe

Music, in the best sense, does not require novelty; nay, the older it is, and the more we are accustomed to it, the greater its effect.

Johann Wolfgang von Goethe

Music is the fourth great material want of our nature,—first food, then raiment, then shelter, then music.

Christian Nestell Bovee

Preposterous ass! that never read so far to know the cause why music was ordained! Was it not to refresh the mind of man, after his studies, or his usual pain?

William Shakespeare

Music is the art of the prophets, the only art that can calm the agitations of the soul; it is one of the most magnificent and delightful presents God has given us.

Martin Luther

Music is the medicine of the breaking heart.

Alfred William Hunt

Music, once admitted to the soul, becomes a sort of spirit, and never dies. It wanders perturbedly through the halls and galleries of the memory, and is often heard again, distinct and living as when it first displaced the wavelets of the air.

Edward George Bulwer-Lytton

It is in learning music that many youthful hearts learn to love.

Dominique Ricard

It calls in my spirits, composes my thoughts, delights my ears, recreates my mind, and so not only fits me for after business, but fills my heart, at the present, with pure and useful thoughts; so that when the music sounds the sweetest in my ears, truth commonly flows the clearest into my mind.

Bishop William Beveridge

Music is the only sensual gratification in which mankind may indulge to excess without injury to their moral or religious feelings.

Joseph Addison

All musical people seem to be happy; it is to them the engrossing pursuit; almost the only innocent and unpunished passion.

Sydney Smith

Music washes away from the soul the dust of every-day life.
Berthold Auerbach

297

Among the instrumentalities of love and peace, surely there can be no sweeter, softer, more effective voice than that of gentle peace-breathing music.

Elihu Burritt

Music is a discipline, and a mistress of order and good manners, she makes the people milder and gentler, more moral and more reasonable.

Martin Luther

There's no music in a "rest," but there's the making of music in it. And people are always missing that part of the life melody, always talking of perseverance and courage and fortitude; but patience is the finest and worthiest part of fortitude, and the rarest, too.

John Ruskin

Music moves us, and we know not why; we feel the tears, but cannot trace their source. Is it the language of some other state, born of its memory? For what can wake the soul's strong instinct of another world like music?

Letita Elizabeth Landon

Music is the language of praise and one of the most essential preparations for eternity is delight in praising God; a higher acquirement, I do think, than even delight and devotedness in prayer.

Thomas Chalmers

Lord, what music hast thou provided for thy saints in heaven, when thou affordest bad men such music on earth!

Izaak Walton

Next to theology I give to music the highest place and honor. And we see how David and all the saints have wrought their godly thoughts into verse, rhyme, and song.

Martin Luther

Music is a prophecy of what life is to be; the rainbow of promise translated out of seeing into hearing.

Lydia M. Child

The lines of poetry, the periods of prose, and even the texts of Scripture most frequently recollected and quoted, are those which are felt to be pre-eminently musical.

William Shenstone

Life is like music, it must be composed by ear, feeling and instinct, not by rule. Nevertheless one had better know the rules, for they sometimes guide in doubtful cases, though not often.

Samuel Butler

Music is the child of prayer, the companion of religion.

Francois René Chateaubriand

Music wakes the soul, and lifts it high, and wings it with sublime desires, and fits it to bespeak the Deity.

Joseph Addison

We love music for the buried hopes, the garnered memories, the tender feelings it can summon at a touch.

Letitia Elizabeth Landon

CHARACTERISTICS OF SUCCESS

A man may be outwardly successful all his life long, and die hollow and worthless as a puff-ball; and he may be externally defeated all his life long, and dies in the royalty of a kingdom established within him—A man's true estate of power and riches, is to be in himself; not in his dwelling, or position, or external relations, but in his own essential character.—That is the realm in which he is to live, if he is to live as a Christian man.

Henry Ward Beecher

A man is one whose body has been trained to be the ready servant of his mind; whose passions are trained to be the servants of his will; who enjoys the beautiful, loves truth, hates wrong, loves to do good, and respects others as himself.

John Ruskin

Contemporaries appreciate the man rather than the merit; but posterity will regard the merit rather than the man.

Caleb C. Colton

You cannot dream yourself into a character; you must hammer and forge one for yourself.

James A. Froude

You may deceive all the people part of the time, and part of the people all the time, but not all the people all the time.

Abraham Lincoln

Character is the real foundation of all worthwhile success.

John Hays Hammond

It is not what a man gets, but what a man is, that he should think of.—He should think first of his character, and then of his condition: for if he have the former, he need have no fears about the latter.—Character will draw condition after it.— Circumstances obey principles.

Henry Ward Beecher

He who acts wickedly in private life, can never be expected to show himself noble in public conduct. He that is base at home, will not acquit himself with honor abroad; for it is not the man but only the place that is changed.

Eschines

Change is one thing, progress is another. "Change" is scientific, "progress" is ethical; change is indisputable, whereas progress is a matter of controversy.

Bertrand Russell

The heart has eyes that the brain knows nothing.

Charles Henry Parkhurst

The best characters are made by vigorous and persistent resistance to evil tendencies; whose amiability has been built upon the ruins of ill-temper, and whose generosity springs from an overmastered and transformed selfishness. Such a character, built up in the presence of enemies, has far more attraction than one which is natively pleasing.

Henry Martyn Dexter

A good character is, in all cases, the fruit of personal exertion. It is not inherited from parents; it is not created by external advantages; it is no necessary appendage of birth, wealth, talents, or station; but it is the result of one's own endeavors—the fruit and reward of good principles manifested in a course of virtuous and honorable action.

Joel Hawes

If you would create something, you must be something.

Johann Wolfgang von Goethe

Modesty seldom resides in a breast that is not enriched with nobler virtues.

Oliver Goldsmith

In the destiny of every moral being there is an object more worthy of God than happiness.—It is character.—And the grand aim of man's creation is the development of a grand character— and grand character is, by its very nature, the product of probationary discipline.

Austin Phelps

Not education, but character, is man's greatest need and man's greatest safeguard.

Herbert Spencer

There is a broad distinction between character and reputation, for one may be destroyed by slander, while the other can never be harmed save by its possessor. Reputation is in no man's keeping. You and I cannot determine what other men shall think and say about us. We can only determine what they ought to think of us and say about us.

Josiah Gilbert Holland

To be worth anything, character must be capable of standing firm upon its feet in the world of daily work, temptation, and trial; and able to bear the wear and tear of actual life. Cloistered virtues do not count for much.

Samuel Smiles

The character that needs law to mend it, is hardly worth the tinkering.

Douglas Jerrold

How little do they see what really is, who frame their hasty judgment upon that which seems.

Robert Southey

Judge thyself with the judgment of sincerity, and thou wilt judge others with the judgment of charity.

John Mason

Men are not to be judged by their looks, habits, and appearances; but by the character of their lives and conversations, and by their works.—It is better to be praised by one's own works than by the words of another.

Sir Roger L'Estrange

Character and personal force are the only investments that are worth anything.

Walt Whitman

The greatest ornament of an illustrious life is modesty and humility, which go a great way in the character even of the most exalted princes.

Napoleon Bonaparte

Who can refute a sneer?—It is independent of proof, reason, argument, or sense, and may as well be used against facts and truth, as against falsehood.

Charles Simmons

To know how to wait is the great secret of success.

Joseph Marie De Maistre

Simple words, short maxims, homely truths, old sayings, are the masters of the world. In them is the hiding of the power that forms the character, controls conduct, and makes individuals, and nations what they are. Great reformations, great revolutions in society, great eras in human progress and improvement, start words, right words, sound words, spoken in the fitting time, and finding their way to human hearts as easily as the birds find their homes.

Daniel March

It is not what he has, or even what de does which expresses the worth of a man, but what he is.

Henri Frederic Amiel

Licentiousness.—Impure thoughts waken impure feelings, lead to impure expressions, and beget impure actions, and these lead to imbecility both of body and mind, and to the ruin of all that is noble and pure in character.

Charles Simmons

The style shows the man. Whether in speaking or writing, a gentleman is always known by his style.

From the Latin

A musician must make music, an artist must paint, a poet must write, if he is to be ultimately at peace with himself. What a man can be, he must be.

Abraham H. Maslow

He is a good man whose intimate friends are all good, and whose enemies are decidedly bad.

John Caspar Lavater

It is not ease but effort,—not facility, but difficulty, that makes men. There is, perhaps, no station in life in which difficulties have not to be encountered and overcome before any decided measure of success can be achieved.

Samuel Smiles

To see what is right, and not do it, is want of courage, or of principle.

Confucius

A good heart, benevolent feelings, and a balanced mind, lie at the foundation of character. Other things may be deemed fortuitous; they may come and go; but character is that which lives and abides, and is admired long after its possessor has left the earth.

John Todd

We sometimes meet an original gentleman, who, if manners had not existed, would have invented them.

Ralph Waldo Emerson

Failure is, in a sense, the highway to success, inasmuch as every discovery of what is false leads us to seek earnestly after what is true, and every fresh experience points out some form of error which we shall afterward carefully avoid.

John Keats

Strong passions are the life of manly virtues. But they need not necessarily be evil because they are passions, and because they are strong. They may be likened to blood horses, that need training and the curb only, to enable those whom they carry to achieve the most glorious triumphs.

William Gilmore Simms

An inexhaustible good nature is one of the most precious gifts of heaven, spreading itself like oil over the troubled sea of thought, and keeping the mind smooth and equable in the roughest weather.

Washington Irving

As you say, I am honoured and famous and rich. But as I have to do all the hard work, and suffer an increasing multitude of fools gladly, it does not feel any better than being reviled, infamous and poor, as I used to be.

George Bernard Shaw

Devote each day to the object then in time, and every evening will find something done.

Johann Wolfgang von Goethe

People seem not to see that their opinion of the world is also a confession of character.

Ralph Waldo Emerson

A really great man is known by three signs—generosity in the design, humanity in the execution, moderation in success.

Otto Eduard Bismarck

A strenuous soul hates cheap success; it is the ardor of the assailant that makes the vigor of the defendant.

Ralph Waldo Emerson

The greatest man is he who chooses the right with invincible resolution; who resists the sorest temptations from within and without; who bears the heaviest burdens cheerfully; who is calmest in storms and most fearless under menace and frowns; and whose reliance on truth, on virtue, and on God, is most unfaltering.

William Ellery Channing

Everybody finds out, sooner or later, that all success worth having is founded on Christian rules of conduct.

Henry Martin Field

A contemplation of God's works, a generous concern for the good of mankind, and the unfeigned exercise of humility—these only, denominate men great and glorious.

Joseph Addison

Nothing succeeds as well as success.

Alexander A. Talleyrand-Perigord

Character is a diamond that scratches every other stone.

Cyrus A. Bartol

Persistent people begin their success where others end in failure.

Edward Eggleston

None will improve your lot if you yourself do not.

Bertolt Brecht

One of the strongest characteristics of genius is the power of lighting its own fire.

John Foster

Perhaps a gentleman is a rarer man than some of us think for. Which of us can point out many such in his circle; men whose aims are generous, whose truth is not only constant in its kind, but elevated in its degree; whose want of meanness makes them simple, who can look the world honestly in the face with an equal manly sympathy for the great and the small.

William Makepeace Thackeray

Nothing will give permanent success in any enterprise of life, except native capacity cultivated by honest and persevering effort.—Genius is often but the capacity for receiving and improving by discipline.

George Eliot

To become an able and successful man in any profession, three things are necessary: nature, study, and practice.

Anonymous

A failure establishes only this, that our determination to succeed was not strong enough.

Christian Nestell Bovee

Never one thing and seldom one person can make for a success. It takes a number of them merging into one perfect whole.

Marie Dressler

Characters do not change.— Opinions alter, but characters are only developed.
Benjamin Disraeli

The mightiest powers by deepest calms are fed.

Bryan Waller Procter

Success in life is a matter not so much of talent or opportunity as of concentration and perseverance.

Charles William Wendte

Man being made a reasonable, and so a thinking creature, there is nothing more worthy of his being, than the right direction and employment of his thoughts, since upon this depend both his usefulness to the public, and his own present and future benefit in all respects.

William Penn

The greatest assassin of life is haste, the desire to reach things before the right time, which means over-reaching them.

Juan Ramon Jimenez

The surest way not to fail is to determine to succeed.

Richard Brinsley Sheridan

In most things success depends on knowing how long it takes to succeed.

Charles de Secondat Montesquieu

If you light upon an impertinent talker that sticks to you like a burr, deal freely with him, break off the discourse, and pursue your business.

Plutarch

The great thing in this world is not so much where we are, but in what direction we are moving.

Oliver Wendell Holmes

Talkative people who wish to be loved are hated; when they desire to please, they bore; when they think they are admired, they are laughed at; they injure their friends, benefit their enemies, and ruin themselves.

Plutarch

Good nature is the very air of a good mind; the sign of a large and generous soul, and the peculiar soil in which virtue prospers.

Godfrey Goodman

Affability, mildness, tenderness, and a word which I would fain bring back to its original signification of virtue—I mean good nature—are of daily use; they are the bread of mankind and the staff of life.

John Dryden

You cannot build up a character in a solitude; you need a formed character to stand a solitude.

Austin O'Malley

Good nature is the beauty of the mind, and like personal beauty, wins almost without anything else—sometimes, indeed, in spite of positive deficiencies.

Jonas Hanway

There are three kinds of people in the world, the wills, the won'ts and the can'ts. The first accomplish everything; the second oppose everything; the third fail in everything.

Eclectic Magazine

AVAILABLE RESOURCES

The following books, videos, and audiocassettes have been reviewed by the Wade Cook Seminars, Inc. or Lighthouse Publishing Group, Inc. staff and are suggested as reading and resource material for continuing education to help with your financial planning, and real estate and stock market investments. Because new ideas and techniques come along and laws change, we're always updating our catalog.

To order a copy of our current catalog, please write or call:

Wade Cook Seminars, Inc.
14675 Interurban Avenue South
Seattle, Washington 98168-4664
1-800-872-7411

Or, visit us on our web sites at:
www.wadecook.com
www.lighthousebooks.com

Also, we would love to hear your comments on our products and services, as well as your testimonials on how these products have benefited you. We look forward to hearing from you!

AUDIOCASSETTES

Income Formulas-A free cassette
By Wade B. Cook

Learn the II cash flow formulas taught in the Wall Street Workshop. Learn to double some of your money in 2 ½ to 4 months.

Zero To Zillions
By Wade B. Cook

This is a powerful audio workshop on Wall Street-understanding the stock market game, playing it successfully, and retiring rich. Learn II powerful investment strategies to avoid pitfalls and losses, catch "Day-trippers," "Bottom fish," write Covered Calls, double your money in one week on options on stock split companies, and so much more. Wade "Meter Drop" Cook will teach you how he makes fantastic annual returns in your account.

Power Of Nevada Corporations-A free cassette
By Wade B. Cook

Nevada Corporations have secrecy, privacy, minimal taxes, no reciprocity with the IRS, and protection for shareholders, officers, and directors. This is a powerful seminar.

Income Streams-A free cassette
By Wade B. Cook

Learn to buy and sell real estate the Wade Cook way. This informative cassette will instruct you in building and operating your own real estate money machine.

Money Machine I & II
By Wade B. Cook

Learn the benefits of buying, and more importantly, selling real estate. Now the system for creating and maintaining a real estate money machine is available in audiocassette form. Money Machine I & II teach the step by step cash flow formulas that made Wade Cook and thousands like him millions of dollars.

Money Mysteries of the Millionaires-A free cassette
By Wade B. Cook

How to make money and keep it. This fantastic seminar shows you how to use Nevada Corporations, Living Trusts, Pension Plans, Charitable Remainder Trusts, and Family Limited Partnerships to protect your assets.

Unlimited Wealth Audio Set
By Wade B. Cook

Unlimited Wealth is the "University of Money-Making Ideas" home study course that helps you to make more money, pay fewer taxes, and keep more for your retirement and family.

Retirement Prosperity
By Wade B. Cook

Take that IRA money now sitting idle and invest it in ways that generate you bigger, better, and quicker returns. This four audiotape set walks you through a system of using a self directed IRA to create phenomenal profits, virtually tax free!

The Financial Fortress Home Study Course
By Wade B. Cook

This eight-part series helps you structure your business and your affairs so that you can avoid the majority of taxes, retire rich, escape lawsuits, bequeath your assets to your heirs without government interference, and, in short-bomb proof your entire estate.

Paper Tigers and Paper Chase
By Wade B. Cook

Wade gives you a personal introduction to the art of buying and selling real estate. In this set of six cassettes, Wade shares his inside secrets to establishing a cash flow business with real estate investments. You will learn how to find discounted second mortgages, find second mortgage notes and make them better, as well as how you can get 40%-plus yields on your money. Learn the art of structuring your business to attract investors and bring in the income you desire through the use of family corporations, pension plans, and other legal entities. A manual is included.

High Performance Business Strategies
By Wade B. Cook

For years, Wade Cook and his staff have listened to people's questions, and concerns. Because they know that problems are best solved by people who already know the ropes, Wade's staff wanted to help. They categorized the questions and came up with about 60 major areas of concern. Wade then went into the recording studio and dealt head on with these questions. What resulted is a comprehensive collection of knowledge to get you started quickly.

> The money is in the meter drop; you get in, you get out, you make money.
>
> Wade B. Cook

BOOKS

Wall Street Money Machine
By Wade B. Cook

Appearing on the New York Times Business Best Sellers list for over one year, Wall Street Money Machine contains the best strategies for wealth enhancement and cash flow creation you'll find anywhere. Throughout this book, Wade Cook describes many of his favorite strategies for generating cash flow through the stock market: Rolling Stock, Proxy Investing, Covered Calls, and many more. It's a great introduction for creating wealth using the Wade Cook formulas.

Stock Market Miracles
By Wade B. Cook

Stock Market Miracles improves on some of the strategies from Wall Street Money Machine, as well as introducing new and valuable twists on our old favorites. This is a must read for anyone interested in making serious money in the stock market.

Bear Market Baloney
By Wade B. Cook

A more timely book wouldn't be possible. Don't miss this insightful look into what makes bull and bear markets and how to make exponential returns in any market.

Real Estate Money Machine
By Wade B. Cook

Wade's first bestselling book reveals how to make money regardless of the state of the economy. Wade's innovative concepts for investing in real estate not only avoids high interest rates, but avoids banks altogether.

How To Pick Up Foreclosures
By Wade B. Cook

Do you want to become an expert money maker in real estate? This book will show you how to buy real estate at 60¢ on the dollar or less. You'll learn to find the house before the auction and purchase it with no bank financing-the easy way to millions in real estate. The market for foreclosures is a tremendous place to learn and prosper. How To Pick Up Foreclosures takes Wade's methods from Real Estate Money Machine and super charges them by applying the fantastic principles to already-discounted properties.

Owner Financing
By Wade B. Cook

This is a short but invaluable booklet you can give to sellers who hesitate to sell you their property using the owner financing method. Let this pamphlet convince both you and them. The special report, "Why Sellers Should Take Monthly Payments," is included for free!

Real Estate For Real People
By Wade B. Cook

A priceless, comprehensive overview of real estate investing, this book teaches you how to buy the right property for the right price, at the right time. Wade Cook explains all of the strategies you'll need, and gives you 20 reasons why you should start investing in real estate today. Learn how to retire rich with real estate, and have fun doing it.

101 Ways To Buy Real Estate Without Cash
By Wade B. Cook

Wade Cook has personally achieved success after success in real estate. 101 Ways To Buy Real Estate Without Cash fills the gap left by other authors who have given all the ingredients but not the whole recipe for real estate investing. This is the book for the investor who wants innovative and practical methods for buying real estate with little or no money down.

Blueprints for Success, Volume I
Contributors: Wade Cook, Debbie Losse, Joel Black, Dan Wagner, Tim Semingson, Rich Simmons, Greg Witt, JJ Childers, Keven Hart, Dave Wagner and Steve Wirrick

Blueprints For Success, Volume I is a compilation of chapters on building your wealth through your business and making your business function successfully. The chapters cover: education and information gathering, choosing the best business for you from all the different types of business, and a variety of other skills necessary for becoming successful. Your business can't afford to miss out on these powerful insights!

Brilliant Deductions
By Wade B. Cook

Learn how to get rich in spite of the updated 1997 tax laws. See new tax credits, year-end maneuvers, and methods for transferring and controlling your entities. Learn to structure yourself and your family for tax savings and liability protection. Available in bookstores or call our toll free number: 1-800-872-7411.

Wealth 101
By Wade B. Cook

This incredible book brings you 101 strategies for wealth creation and protection that you can't afford to miss. Front to back, it is packed full of tips and tricks to supercharge your financial health. If you need to generate more cash flow, this book shows you how through several various avenues. If you are already wealthy, this is the book that will show you strategy upon strategy for decreasing your tax liability and increasing your peace of mind through liability protection.

> Y ou can't go broke making a profit.
>
> Wade B. Cook

VIDEOS

Dynamic Dollars Video
By Wade B. Cook

Wade Cook's 90 minute introduction to the basics of his Wall Street formulas and strategies. In this presentation designed especially for video, Wade explains the meter drop philosophy, Rolling Stock, basics of Proxy Investing, and writing Covered Calls. Perfect for anyone looking for a little basic information.

The Wall Street Workshop Video Series
By Wade B. Cook

Ten albums containing 11 hours of intense instruction on Rolling Stock, options on stock split companies, writing Covered Calls, and eight other tested and proven strategies. By learning, reviewing, and implementing the strategies taught here, you will gain the knowledge and the confidence to take control of your investments, and get your money to work hard for you.

The Next Step Video Series
By Team Wall Street

The advanced version of the Wall Street Workshop. Full of power-packed strategies from Wade Cook, this is not a duplicate of the Wall Street Workshop, but a very important partner. The methods taught in this seminar will supercharge the strategies taught in the Wall Street Workshop and teach you even more ways to make more money!

In The Next Step, you'll learn how to find the stocks to fit the formulas through technical analysis, fundamentals, home trading tools, and more.

Build Perpetual Income (BPI)-A videocassette

Wade Cook Seminars, Inc. is proud to present Build Perpetual Income, the latest in our ever-expanding series of seminar home study courses. In this video, you will learn powerful real estate cash-flow generating techniques, such as:

- Power negotiating strategies

- Buying and selling mortgages

- Writing contracts

- Finding and buying discount properties

- Avoiding debt

> You can't get lucky if you're not in the game.
>
> Wade B. Cook

Classes Offered

Cook University

People enroll in Cook University for a variety of reasons. Usually they are a little discontented with where they are-their job is not working, their business is not producing the kind of income they want, or they definitely see that they need more income to prepare for a better retirement. That's where Cook University comes in.

The backbone of the one-year program is the Money Machine concept-as applied to your business, to stock investments, or to real estate. Although there are many, many other forms of investing in real estate, there are really only three that work: the Money Machine method, buying second mortgages, and lease options. Of these three, the Money Machine stands head and shoulders above the rest.

Perpetual monthly income is waiting. We'll teach you how to achieve it. We'll show you how to make it. We'll watch over you while you're making it happen. We hope to see you in the program right away.

IF YOU WANT TO BE WEALTHY, THIS IS THE PLACE TO BE.

The Wall Street Workshop
Presented by Wade B. Cook and Team Wall Street

The Wall Street Workshop teaches you how to make incredible money in all markets. It teaches you the tried-and-true strategies that have made hundreds of people wealthy.

The Next Step Workshop
Presented by Wade B. Cook and Team Wall Street

An Advanced Wall Street Workshop designed to help those ready to take their trading to the next level and treat it as a business. This seminar is open only to graduates of the Wall Street Workshop.

Executive Retreat
Presented by Wade B. Cook and Team Wall Street

Created especially for the individuals already owning or planning to establish Nevada Corporations, the Executive Retreat is a unique opportunity for corporate executives to participate in workshops geared toward streamlining operations and maximizing efficiency and impact.

Wealth Institute
Presented by Wade B. Cook and Team Wall Street

This three day workshop defines the art of asset protection and entity planning. During these three days we will discuss, in depth and detail, the six domestic entities which will protect you from lawsuits, taxes, or other financial losses, and help you retire rich.

Real Estate Workshop
Presented by Wade B. Cook and Team Main Street

The Real Estate Workshop teaches you how to build perpetual income for life, without going to work. Some of the topics include buying and selling paper, finding discounted properties, generating long-term monthly cash flow, and controlling properties wihtout owning them.

Real Estate Bootcamp
Presented by Wade B. Cook and Team Main Street

This three to four day Bootcamp is truly a roll-up-your-sleeves-and-do-the-deals event. You will be learning how to locate the bargains, negotiate strategies, and find wholesale properties (pre-foreclosures). You will also visit a title company, look at properties and learn some new and fun selling strategies.

Business Entity Skills Training (BEST)
Presented by Wade B. Cook and Team Wall Street

Learn about the six powerful entities you can use to protect your wealth and your family. Learn the secrets of asset protection, eliminate your fear of litigation, and minimize your taxes.

You have to know your exit before ever going in the entrance.

Wade B. Cook

ASSORTED RESOURCES

Wealth Information Network (WIN)

This subscription Internet service provides you with the latest financial formulas and updated entity structuring strategies. New, timely information is entered Monday through Friday, sometimes four or five times a day. Wade Cook and his Team Wall Street staff write for WIN, giving you updates on their own current stock plays, companies who announced earnings, companies who announced stock splits, and the latest trends in the market.

WIN is also divided into categories according to specific strategies and contains archives of all our trades so you can view our history. If you are just getting started in the stock market, this is a great way to follow people who are doubling their money every 2½ to 4 months. If you are experienced already, it's the way to confirm your feelings and research with others who are generating wealth through the stock market.

IQ Pager

This is a system which beeps you as events and announcements are made on Wall Street. With IQ Pager, you'll receive information about events like major stock split announcements, earnings surprises, important mergers and acquisitions, judgements or court decisions involving big companies, important bankruptcy announcements, big winners and losers, and disasters. If you're getting your financial information from the evening news, you're getting it too late. The key to the stock market is timing. Especially when you're trading in options, you need up-to-the-minute (or second) information. You cannot afford to sit at a computer all day looking for news or wait for your broker to call. IQ Pager is the ideal partner to the Wealth Information Network (WIN).

The Incorporation Handbook
By Wade B. Cook

Incorporation made easy! This handbook tells you who, why, and, most importantly, how to incorporate. Included are samples of the forms you will use when you incorporate, as well as a step-by-step guide from the experts.

Legal Forms
By Wade B. Cook

This collection of pertinent forms contains numerous legal forms used in real estate transactions. These forms were selected by experienced investors, but are not intended to replace the advice of an attorney. However, they will provide essential forms for you to follow in your personal investing.

Quit tripping over pennies on your way to dollars.

Wade B. Cook

AUTHOR INDEX

A

B

H

N